"Everyone has a story within their history, and everyone has the power to make it a testimony of grace and possibility. Lisa Kai has done exactly that. In her first book, "Perfectly You", she's shares with honesty and transparency the challenges of being a young girl raised in a different land and culture to one she now calls home. I have known Lisa and her husband Mike for many years now, and as they have lent into God's heart for their own lives and ministry, I have watched the call of God flourish in all she touches. She has a tangible desire to help people and especially the women of her own planting in Hawaii. I am confident this book will enlighten and inspire you and be something that you will eagerly share with others."

−BOBBIE HOUSTON, *Hillsong Church*

"I love Lisa! That is one of the many reasons I'm so thrilled that she has taken the time to pen Perfectly You. I know that on these pages you will fall in love with her too as she takes you on a journey to freedom and purpose. Lisa gives you permission to be "beautiful, accepted, honored, brave, bold, and loved" because "we no longer have to be fearful, intimidated, or perfect" to become exactly who Christ says we are!"

−LISA BEVERE, *New York Times Best-Selling Author - Without Rival, Lioness Arising, and Girls With Swords*

"Lisa has lived this book. She is an inspiration to those of us who are wondering how we can break the bonds of insecurity and intimidation. Throughout the years of friendship, I've had with her, she truly continues to arise and break through barriers in her own life and in turn help others to do so in their lives. This book will inspire you to run in your lane and be comfortable in your own skin - to be perfectly you."

—ANDI ANDREW - Lead Pastor, Liberty Church, NYC

"Lisa Kai is an incredible human being whom I love and admire and have had the honor of knowing over 25 years. I've watched her swoop in person after person and take them off the bench and put them on the field without them even knowing it! As you turn each page you'll see what I love about Lisa: a woman with finesse and fire passionately mixed to see you live out... Perfectly You."

—TISHA LEHFELDT - Radio Host, 95.5 The Fish

"Irrespective of who you are, insecurity and self-worth attempt to dissettle us at the minimum and eradicate us at the maximum. This book exposes the tactics of the enemy and encourages us to RISE UP to our full potential in Jesus! I loved this book! I would whole heartedly exhort all would-be leaders to read the heart of Lisa Kai."

—TINA ARCHER - Lead Pastor, Puyallup Foursquare Church, Puyallup, Washington)

"Perfectly You" is Lisa Kai's story of the various seasons she has walked through. Whether you are a stay at home mum, a college student, a business woman or someone in church leadership, you will be grateful for Lisa's authenticity as she shares her journey and encourages you to step out of your comfort zone and be all that God has destined you to be. It's been my joy to watch this great lady live out the principles outlined in this book."

—LYN ALCORN, Senior Pastor, Hope Centre

"Lisa has brilliantly, in such a raw and real way communicated the angst every woman in leadership faces. Whatever arena you find yourself in, this book will undoubtedly help you navigate and pursue all that God has purposed in your heart. This is a must read for every woman regardless of age, background or status!!!! Congratulations and well done Lisa for hitting it out of the park!"

–PASTOR SHARON KELLY, Wave Church, Virginia Beach, VA.

"Lisa's journey and her understanding on the subject of identity and breaking through insecurity will help you unlock your hidden potential. Finding out who God created you to be will be your greatest discovery ever. Search for it with all your heart. 'Perfectly You' will be perfect for you."

–LEIGH RAMSEY, Senior Pastor - Citipointe Church, Brisbane

"Lisa Kai is the genuine article. In all the years I've known her she has always been 'straight up' and truthful - it is one of her strongest qualities. As she shares her own journey to personal freedom in equally raw and honest style, I believe it will help many others to find their footing and the courage needed to carve their own path forward into confidence and fruitfulness in life."

–GEORGIE BAXTER, Enjoy Church, Australia

perfectly
you

Get Set Free from Insecurity
and Become Exactly Who
God Created You to Be

LISA KAI

emerge
publishing
TULSA OKLAHOMA

Published by:

TULSA, OKLAHOMA

Emerge Publishing, LLC
9521B Riverside Parkway, Suite 243
Tulsa, Oklahoma 74137
Phone: 888.407.4447
www.EmergePublishing.com

Library of Congress Cataloging-in-Publication Data

ISBN: 978-1-943127-49-8 Paperback
ISBN: 978-1-943127-50-4 Digital/E-book

BISAC Category:
REL012130 RELIGION / Christian Life / Women's Issues
SEL023000 SELF-HELP / Personal Growth / Self-Esteem

Printed in the United States of America.

TABLE OF CONTENTS

DEDICATION

I dedicate this book to my husband, Mike, and to my girls, Courtney, Rebekah-Taylor and Charis. Thank you for loving and believing in me to fulfill all God has asked me to do. It's been quite a journey, and I thank God we did this together. Girls, I pray that you will take the truths from this book and pass them on to your children and to your grandchildren. My life has been enlarged and filled with purpose because I said yes to Jesus. I want you, girls, to keep loving and serving Jesus all the days of your life. Dad and I are so proud to be your parents, and we always strive to teach you who Jesus is and to be a good example of what it means to be a servant of Jesus.

Thank you, Mike, for always loving and encouraging me to stretch beyond my capacity. I am a blessed woman because you love me so well! I couldn't have written this book without your help. I can't wait to do more with you as we continue to pastor Inspire Church together with an amazing team that God has gathered for us to lead.

A special thank you to my friend Krystie Gonzales for pushing me year after year to write this book and for editing my first draft. I also want to thank Inspire Church for being the church that continues to rise up and be everything that God has called us to be. Let's never stop growing as a church. Let's continue to tell our story about what Jesus has done in our lives.

FOREWORD

I love sitting on the front row. Whether it's at a college basketball game and I've been blessed with tickets to sit on the floor and watch my team, or at church listening to God's Word as it is delivered, the front row is my favorite place to sit. There's something to be said about being up close to the action. On the front row, you can hear what the players are saying to one another and you can feel the action. There are things you won't catch sitting higher up or further away. But up close where the players are, you can see what shoes they're wearing and what they say to the opposing teams bench. I find it to be an added dimension to just watching from what many would consider a greater vantage point.

It's in the front row that you can feel the passion and energy. It doesn't matter if it's a concert, a church service or a conference. In fact, my pastor used to comment about me as a young believer that I always wanted to sit in the front row. There I would notice what he was wearing that day and even try to get a glimpse of his preaching notes. He once told me, "It's because you like being closer to the fire." I would have to say that there's nothing like being on the front row.

I'm sure Lisa could have asked a woman to write this foreword and it might have been more appropriate considering we have come to know some amazing women who have preached on greater platforms and pastored longer that she and I have together. These women have had a tremendous impact on her life. But when push came to shove and the date of printing drew nearer, Lisa suggested that I be the one to write the foreword for this book.

I gave it some thought and then I realized that I have had the privilege of watching her life unfold from a "front row" vantage point. Not only have we been married for over 23 years, but I have also watched her blossom before my very eyes from a shy, somewhat reluctant pastor's wife, to the person she is today. I have watched her fight through her reluctance to change and allow the Lord to mold and shape her like clay on the wheel at the hands of the Potter. There have been many times when she doubted herself, her abilities and the call of God on her life to the point of early-mornings on her knees, tears in her eyes as she asked for His presence before she would get up to speak.

Like most of us, she was held captive by the insecurities of her ethnic culture, and the environment in which she was raised. Without taking anything away from my in-laws whom I love and respect dearly, growing up in Hawai'i as a first-generation immigrant was not easy for Lisa and her siblings. But as they have all forged their own paths in this world, she was the first to come to faith in Jesus. From that moment on, Lisa has had to fight through spiritual resistance. As a single, Christian woman trying to live a set-apart life, she matured in her relationship with Jesus. And now, as a middle-aged mother and grandmother (the most gorgeous, I might add), she has experienced this metamorphosis to arise and inspire women from Hawai'i and literally across the globe. I guess we could call her "the accidental leader" of a movement of women. But then she would be quick to say that by no means is she the first (because she isn't) nor will she be the last. As the saying goes, "we all stand on the shoulders of giants", and we do. She did not ask for this to happen, nor did she strive for it. But rather, Lisa has accepted it and is continuing, day-by-day, to walk in her calling. God has truly graced her to do this and I have been honored to witness this transformation first-hand.

Perfectly You is her story. It has become our story. But I truly believe that it is also the story of many of you reading this. I did not help Lisa write this book, but only gave encouragement and just a small bit of help in representing facts and situations more clearly only when she asked me to. As you will come to pleasantly discover, Lisa has an innocent, unassuming way about her that is evident in her writing style, yet at the same time, she is filled with Godly-wisdom and grace in all she does. In many ways, Lisa is just as I first met her, which makes me adore her even more. But she is certainly not the same. She has been blessed every step of the way, and given the grace to persevere to this day. God's hand is on her life is so evident and it is an honor to watch from the front row.

I encourage you to read this book over a cup of coffee, or at your favorite beach spot. Get alone with God and allow the Holy Spirit to speak to you. Laugh at her candor and identify with her stories as this is not an exegetical thesis on the "calling of God on your life" (insert baritone voice here) but the story of a wife, mother, sister, daughter and a friend who just said "Yes, Lord! I don't want to, but I will do it!" (imagine her tearful cries?) and who eventually did it. Be inspired but more importantly, learn to become *perfectly you*, because that's exactly what the Lord desires to accomplish through this book.

Mike Kai
January, 2017

INTRODUCTION

Have you ever felt a shift happening inside of you that awakened something, and you couldn't explain it or shake it off, but you knew God was trying to get your attention? I believe God is trying to get our attention today because He has so much to say to His children, if only we would listen. He has been beckoning His children to come home, rise up and know our calling because He has plans and purposes that He wants to fulfill in us and through us.

> *"If ever the Church needed to be dangerous and fully awake, the time is now!"*
> **-Lisa Bevere**

As I was awakened from my slumber, it was like an alarm clock had gone off. I heard a trumpet sound, but I didn't understand what it meant. All I knew was that I had been asking God what my next season would look like and that I was ready to do whatever He wanted me to do. I wanted to make an impact with what God has given to my husband, Mike and I, and our church. I was ready to work.

As I answered His call to lead the women's ministry, I struggled with so many insecurities and fears that held me back from rising up. Have you ever been sick and tired of the fears and insecurities that battle inside of you, that often hold you back from being fully who you were intended to be? I wanted to overcome these insecurities and fears, and it was a process and a journey that I was willing to take.

We often will ask ourselves these questions: is there more to life than what I am doing right now? What does my next season look like? What am I supposed to be doing with my life? Am I using the gifting that God has given me to make an impact while I am here on earth? How do I overcome the lies that I have believed for so long about myself and walk in the truth of who God says *I AM?* How do I become bold, fearless, brave, and walk in **Godfidence** (God confidence) and not in my own confidence? How do I just be *ME?*

Everyone has a story to tell, and I love to hear these stories because they tell me so much more about who people are, where they came from, and where they are today. Our lives are like books whose chapters tell of the great things we've done and learned in this life, along with the trials and regrets too. That's what makes a great book – it tells all. I'm finally being obedient in writing my story after five years of talking myself out of it.

I love sitting across from so many women, sipping my many Chai lattes with all soy, no water and foam, seven pumps of Chai, extra hot (women are so complicated when ordering their drinks) and hearing their stories. I love it, because I love discovering how God has rescued them, and celebrating what God has done in their lives. I have also sat across from women who have wanted to share their personal story – struggles in their marriages, with their parents, siblings, children, or just with themselves. Every one of these women that I've met, young and old, have the same struggles.

Their struggles are about finding out who they are, what they were created for, and how to overcome their insecurities.

Many men and women struggle with their identity and insecurities, and I believe that when we recognize our insecurities and expose them, we can be set free from them. I've learned over the years that I was tired of faking it. What I mean is that I would look confident and as though I have it all together, when deep inside of me I was struggling with confidence. I get uncomfortable around certain kinds of people and so I compensated my insecurities by faking my confidence, appearing as if I have it all together. I'm sure you don't do that. Yeah right. It's so funny that now, after having to learn how to overcome my insecurities, I can see them in other people. I can tell when someone is faking it with me. I can tell when they are struggling inside because they look a little uncomfortable, or they try to ignore me or won't even approach me. I get this a lot in church because I am the wife of the senior pastor, and that alone usually intimidates people. I remember approaching a woman named Evie but as I introduced myself to her, she seemed very uncomfortable, as if she wanted to run away from me. She couldn't really look me in the eye as we were chatting, and she kept touching her hair like she was nervous. Because I knew that she was feeling intimidated, I tried my best to make her feel comfortable.

Women are so funny; we tend to compare ourselves to one another and compete with one another without the other person knowing we're doing it. I am writing this book, because I can totally relate to those who are dealing with insecurities and their identity. There are two parts to this book. Part One will tell you who I am and where I came from. Part Two will tell you how my journey began as I realized the lies that I had believed about myself that caused me to be insecure and confused about my identity, how I learned to manage those insecurities and overcome my fears.

I believe that as you read this book, you will find freedom in knowing who you are in Christ, and you will want to rise up to your full expression in Him! My prayer is that every one of us will awaken from our sleep and realize the greatest potential lies inside of us. I don't want anyone to miss out on what God is doing here on this earth. I want us to be a company of women who will forcefully advance His kingdom here on the earth. We will no longer sit on the sidelines and watch others do it. We are all called and chosen people of God with an assignment to take the gospel to the ends of the earth. We are all positioned; we just need to take those positions and rise up!

So let me tell you how this journey began. It didn't start in Honolulu; it started way back as a little child in Hong Kong.

PART ONE

A NEW LIFE

CHAPTER ONE

THE JOURNEY BEGINS

"A journey of a thousand miles begins with a single step."   **Lao Tzu**

"The steps of a good man are ordered by the Lord: and he delighteth in his way."   **Psalms 37:23**

Have you ever felt like you were not good enough or that you didn't measure up to the people around you? Have you ever been intimidated by a certain race of people or gender, or by someone who is more popular than you are, or with status? Growing up, I was taught to believe that white people were more powerful than Asian people, and that in order to be successful in life you had to be smart and white.

My parents and I emigrated from Hong Kong when I was one year old. My parents are originally from Canton, China, and they moved to Hong Kong after getting married. Their marriage was arranged by their mothers. You probably thought that doesn't happen anymore, but it still does. My father had the privilege of attending school while his sisters did not. His sisters had to work all of their lives to support the one son who would one day make enough money for the whole family. My mom was not educated because she came from a very poor family. She worked in the rice fields picking rice. To this day, my mom expects us to eat every grain of rice that is on our plate. She reminds us about how hard people work to pick those rice grains. My parents both came from Buddhist families; therefore, we were Buddhist.

My older sister, brother, and I were born in Hong Kong, and my younger sister was born in Hawai'i. We came to Hawai'i like many immigrants looking for a better life for their families. We did not speak English, so my parents' friends had to translate for us as we went through our immigration process. My first language was Cantonese. My oldest sister, Janet, was smart and was the first one to attend school. We all relied on her to communicate for us, as well as translate what had been said. I remember when I started attending school and didn't realize that I was in a classroom with other students, who like me, could not speak or understand English. I didn't think anything of it. I didn't think that I was different from all of the other kids until my second or third year of school. I wondered why I wasn't in the same class with my friends because I was sent to a different class that didn't have many kids in it. We played games such as Concentration and Go Fish. It was fun, I guess, because I still remember it today. But in the second grade I realized that I was different from all the other girls in my class. It didn't feel good. I felt like I was an outcast because I was Chinese and didn't speak that well. Thank God I had an English name given to me when I got my U.S. citizenship. Imagine being called "Gee Fun" in an all-American school. I don't think my friends knew what class I was attending, or maybe they knew, but something inside of me was ashamed and embarrassed. I was embarrassed being Chinese, and I was ashamed that I wasn't progressing like the other normal kids.

As I moved into the third grade, I no longer needed to attend that special class. Hallelujah! I did miss playing those cards games though. I was with everyone my age, doing the same assignments, and it felt good. I was definitely better in math than in English or History. I finally had some friends to play with during recess and friends to sit with during lunch. I was a very impressionable girl; I noticed things about people, like whether they were the popular kids or the kids that were considered weird. There was this girl named Cheryl, and it seemed like everyone liked being around her. In fact, she could have her choice of friends to sit on her right or on her left during lunch. My goal was to be one of the girls sitting on either side. So weird!! I remember asking her daily if I could sit on either side. I believe I had the opportunity to sit on her left side one day and I said to myself, "Wow I made it! I got to sit next to the most popular girl!"

As I look back, I was trying to hide my inadequacies and my shame of being different from all of them. I wanted to be accepted by those that were considered popular or cool.

I had another group of friends that I would hang out with, and they were smart girls, but they weren't as popular as Cheryl. In fact, she was not as smart as my other friends. Maybe that was why I wanted to be with her; she may have been like me, not as smart, but she was popular and I wasn't.

That was a trying time in my life; A foreign girl trying to be accepted by her peers as she pretended to be like them, when in fact she wasn't. I tried so hard to hide my identity as a Chinese immigrant with Chinese-speaking parents. I used to be ashamed of my parents because they represented the person I was trying so hard not to be. I remember when they spoke to me in Chinese in public; I would ignore them as if they were talking to someone else. I did not embrace my heritage or who I was or where I came from. I wanted to be like everyone else. I wanted to be thought of as normal.

Growing up as a teen wasn't easier. I spoke English more than I spoke Cantonese and was doing well in school, but I still didn't appreciate who I was.

As I said, I was very impressionable. I wanted to be like everyone else. I joined the orchestra and played viola for three years and later got into tennis. I even tried out for cheerleading, and I couldn't believe I made the squad. I thought for sure, now I was popular – I was a cheerleader for McKinley High School. Go Tigers! I was also a "key club sweetheart" with my friend, Jamie. If you're wondering what that is, all I can say is that we were the mascots for an all-boys club. I'll be honest, the guys weren't the kind of guys that were on the football or soccer teams; they were more like the band geeks. All we did was attend their functions and smile.

Life was good in high school, and I had the time of my life doing things I never thought I would do. After high school, I went off to a junior college to study tourism, and while I was at junior college, I noticed a poster seeking contestants for the Miss Chinatown Pageant. As a little girl we attended every Chinese New Year festivity, and I was always amazed at the Miss Narcissus and Miss Chinatown courts. So when I saw that poster, I wanted to compete in the pageant. This was probably the only time I was proud to be Chinese because you had to have a certain percentage of Chinese ethnicity in order to participate, as well as a Chinese name. I shocked everyone in my family when I told them I was running for this pageant. I ended up placing second runner-up and won a free round-trip ticket to China and another to Europe. Not bad for a girl who did not honour her heritage.

During college I worked and often went to night clubs with friends. I have to say it was fun, and that's where I met my first boyfriend. We dated and soon lived together for about five years. Ironically, he was the first person to introduce me to Jesus. He was not the best model of a Christian. But I remember attending a bible study with him several times and church on Sundays once in a while whenever he felt like it. Because I was raised as a Buddhist, I proclaimed myself to be Buddhist because my family was Buddhist. I didn't understand the Buddhist religion and I also didn't understand Christianity. The only knowledge I had of Jesus was from a play that I went to called "Jesus Christ Superstar." I just knew Jesus was a white guy with a beard who wore a white robe.

My boyfriend and I broke up several times during our courtship because he often felt convicted about dating a non-Christian and for doing things we weren't supposed to be doing. Each time we broke up and got back together didn't help me to understand who Jesus was. In fact, I was jealous of Jesus because I felt that my boyfriend was more in love with Jesus than he was with me. Why would he breakup with me for Jesus? Because of my boyfriend's guilt about not living the life he was called to, he went back and forth between doing drugs and selling them, and drinking a lot. One day, he didn't come home, and this became a norm in our relationship. So finally, we decided to take a break. I thought that we would maybe get back together, but that wasn't the case. I found out that he had been fooling around with another girl, and he was planning to stay with her. This completely rocked my world because I thought that we were going to get married. During this time, I was completely lost.

CHAPTER TWO

GOD RESCUED ME

"God rescued us from dead end alleys and dark dungeons."　　　　　**Col 1:13 (MSG)**

We broke up and I was heartbroken and lost. At this time I was about 22 years old. I finished college and went to work full-time in the travel industry. I really thought that we were going to get married and have kids and live happily ever after, but that was not the case. In my apartment, I vividly remember sitting at my dining table and looking up and asking this question in my head, "If You want me to go to church, the only way I'll go is if someone invites me." Within five minutes I got a call from my boyfriend's sister wanting to know what was going on with her brother and I. I told her what happened, and right then and there, she asked me "Do you want to go to church with me this Friday?" I looked up to heaven and started to cry because I couldn't believe

God had heard my thoughts. I tried to keep myself from crying on the phone because I didn't want her to know I was crying. I hung up the phone, and my tears just came flooding down my cheeks. I was in awe that God heard and cared about me enough to have someone call and invite me to church. Throughout the week I anxiously waited for Friday because I was going to church! I finally had something to look forward to because I had nothing to look forward to after my breakup except going to work five days a week. Most of my friends at that time were with their boyfriends, so there wasn't much to do in life except work.

I was searching for something, and I guess at that time, I was searching for God. I had come to a place in my life after college where I didn't know what else to do. I had no other purpose than to just work.

I went to church at Hope Chapel Kaneohe Bay (HCKB) that Friday with her, and I was so nervous. I thought, "Oh no, someone is going to know what has happened to me, God is going to know that I had sex, and that I was not a nice person to others." I was so afraid that everyone would know all of the bad things that I had done and was afraid that they may not accept me.

I was filled with anxiety as the usher sat us down. Worship was beginning, and it was very unusual because I wasn't used to that type of music. It was almost like love songs for someone, but they were love songs to God. I sang along with everyone, and I cried and cried and just couldn't stop the tears from flowing. I didn't want anyone to see me crying, so I wiped the tears away as fast as they were flowing. Then the pastor spoke, and I felt like my friend had told him what happened to me. I started to get nervous because I felt like he was speaking directly to my situation. I didn't want anyone to know what had happened to me, and I did not want to be crying in front of these strangers. After he spoke, he asked if anyone wanted to receive Jesus as his or her Lord and Savior, and I knew I wanted Jesus. I raised my hand and I couldn't stop crying. I repeated the prayer and thought, "Is that it? Am I in the "club?" Will I be different now? Will my problems be solved today?" After that prayer, I couldn't believe the peace I felt inside. I did not want the church service to end that night. I wanted to make sure that I was saved; therefore, week after week at church I gave my life to Jesus. My prayer was that Jesus would change me from the inside out because I didn't like the person I was. I didn't see myself as worthy of being a Christian. I had negative and critical thoughts of people, and I used to look down on people who were very different than me. I wanted Jesus to wash me clean; literally wash me like you'd clean something with bleach and water. I wanted Jesus to scrub my heart and give me a new heart. I also wanted God to flush out my entire being of all the junk that was inside of me. Sort of like how women have a menstrual cycle each month when their system needs to be flushed out. That's what I wanted God to do in me.

One of my prayers was to have a new start in life. I wanted a new life with new friends and a new future. I prayed that Jesus would give me friends. I heard someone making an announcement to get involved in a connect group. I didn't know what they were, but I was interested. One night at church, someone invited me to a connect group. If someone had not asked me, I'm not sure if I would have gone to one. I went to my first connect group, or bible study, and it was awesome. I got to meet new people my age, and people who were mature in the faith, and I was able to learn about the bible and how to pray. I remember after our discussion time, we had to break up into groups to pray for one another, and I was not comfortable praying out loud or praying for someone else. I told those in my group that I didn't want to pray, so don't make me.

I did this week after week until one day I asked them, "Can I try to pray?" That connect group was the group of people that helped me learn what it meant to be a Christian. I am forever grateful that God gave me a new life with new friends to do life together. To this day, many of us from that group are pastors and leaders serving the body of Christ.

I remember telling my parents that I was a Christian because they noticed I had been going to church a lot and spending all of my free time there, and noticed the new friends in my life. My mom would often tell me not to completely trust the church or give all of my money away to it. She was worried I was in a cult that just wanted my money. I definitely didn't share with her how much I gave and how much I was supposed to give because she would have gone nuts had I told her. Eventually my parents embraced my new-found faith because they saw how happy I was. I'm sure they sensed more than that, but could not explain it.

After getting connected in the church, I started serving because the pastor said we needed to serve, and when a pastor says we need to serve, we need to serve. I heard they needed help in the children's ministry, so I thought that might be a great place for me to start serving, since the kids didn't know much about the bible and neither did I. That sounded like a good fit for me. I went to help in the 5th/6th grade class, and I dragged my friend Shelly with me. It was fun, and it was there that I learned about David and Goliath, Jonah and the whale, and many more stories that I hadn't heard of. You have to know that I had no background in Christianity at all because of being raised as a Buddhist. So being a Christian was such a new thing for me. I wanted to learn so badly and being with the kids really helped me learn about Jesus.

After I got saved, I decided to go back to school and pursue an education degree. So I quit my full-time job and started to look for a part-time job. I remember praying in my head one morning for a job, and it just so happened that same day, I was at a shopping center parking lot and bumped into a couple of guys who worked for Hope Chapel Kaneohe Bay. It was weird because we all showed up at this place that none of us normally went to. We said hello, and then they asked me if I would like to work for the church. I was blown away again; God heard me and answered my prayers. So I started working for the church part-time as an administrative assistant for the young adults and youth ministry.

A short time later, I was asked to come on full-time as the children's ministry pastor. Now that was totally not what I thought I was going to do in life. I was single and a new believer so you can imagine how I felt. I felt so unworthy to be given this position and totally unqualified. I wasn't a mom, and although I had served in that ministry for a little while, kids weren't my thing. I really didn't like kids, and I had never led anything before. My pastor, Ralph Moore, asked me to pray on this, and I said I would, but I knew the answer would be a "no." It was a no-brainer, but I said I would pray, and I did. In fact, I told my connect group about this, and even they discouraged me from taking the offer.

But something inside of me wasn't settled because there was a sense of my purpose that was attached to this offer. Everything looked like I wasn't qualified to take this position, but for some reason, I felt I was supposed to accept the job. However, because of my fears surrounding the position, I told my pastor that I would not be able to move forward with the job. He didn't like my answer and asked me to pray about it again. I was shocked! He asked me why I wouldn't take it. I told him that I was not qualified, but he said I could learn and that I would do a great job.

That same night at church, we had a guest speaker who shared a message out of Psalm 37. God always speaks to us when He knows we are not listening, and He wanted me to hear Him clearly and used this message to speak to me. In Psalm 37:5, "Commit everything you do to the Lord, trust him, and he will help you." The speaker gave a word picture of a line that is drawn on the ground. Trusting in God is like walking over that line, not knowing what is on the other side. From that moment on, I knew I was supposed to take this job even though I didn't know how to do it or anything about leading a children's ministry. I just had to trust that the Lord would help me. And of course, He helped me lead that ministry for 12 years! During the course of leading the children's ministry, I learned my gift set. I discovered that I was a leader and that I was good at administration. I had a knack for gathering people and putting them in areas where they will flourish. Had I not said yes, I probably would not have known that any of this was my strength.

My life was moving along fine after the breakup. God truly answered my prayer when I asked Him to change my life. I no longer missed my old life; I had a new life with new friends and a church that I had the privilege of working for. I dated a few guys during this new season, but there was one guy that caught my attention. I saw him while I was serving in the children's ministry. I noticed him as he walked past my class with his little girl. I thought he was married, of course, because he had a daughter, so I didn't think anything of it. But I noticed him again by himself with his daughter at a Halloween event we organized for the kids, and I wondered where his wife was. It wasn't until we were at a Christmas party that I actually even learned who he was.

Chapter Three

MEETING MR. RIGHT

We finally met at a singles Christmas party where a hundred other single people were having a great time. I saw him on the dance floor and was observing him while he wasn't looking. He was cute and handsome and seemed like a fun Christian guy. In fact, he looked like a guy on the cover of a romance novel that I used to read as a teenager. He had dark hair and features, with green eyes and an Italian nose. After the party was over, several of us decided to go out to eat, and he and his friend joined us. That was the night that we had a chance to sit next to each other and chat and this is where I first heard his testimony. I noticed his eyes and hair for some reason, and I thought that they were fake. His eyes looked like he was wearing green contact lenses, and I thought his hair was highlighted. I thought he was a pretty boy. Later I asked him if he wore fake contact lenses and highlighted his hair.

He was appalled that I thought they were fake. But I had to ask; if you don't ask, you won't know for sure. That's the kind of girl I am.

I was thinking about him the next day, and thought about inviting him to come with me to a wedding. I was the maid of honor so technically I wouldn't really have sat with him, and he would have had to sit with my friends. I believe that if a guy you're dating can get along with your friends, he is someone you should consider dating. So I called him the day after the party because I had the previous night's Christmas party sign-in sheet with everyone's phone number. I believe that if you want something, you shouldn't be afraid to ask, and it's okay for a girl to call a guy first. My husband says to everyone that I was stalking him because I had the list and I called him first. I just say, "You should thank God I called you because I could have called someone else." So after talking and getting to know him more on the phone, I asked if he would like to attend a wedding with me. I could tell he was a little shocked that a girl asked him out, but he said yes to my invitation and that was the beginning of our courtship.

Mike was a single dad to Courtney and since her mother wasn't in the picture, Mike's parents had helped him raise Courtney from the time she was about two years old. It was a tough break-up for Mike, and biblically speaking, he was faithful to his vows until the very end. That in itself was one of things that attracted me the most to him. He was a committed and loyal guy, who made sure his daughter was well cared for. He had two part-time jobs, working as a valet at a restaurant and at American Airlines. In addition, he had a small Amway business on the side to make ends meet. We hardly dated or saw each another because he was busy with work, and all the extra time he had was spent with his daughter. We saw each other about every two weeks and spoke a lot on the phone. That was our dating life for about three months. We ended up breaking up at a singles camp. We both agreed that things weren't going well with the relationship. I felt that God wasn't at the center of the relationship, and I also believe that it was because we didn't have the time to build our friendship. It was a sad ending to our camp, but we remained friends. In fact, he wrote me a nice long letter expressing his heart for me and how sad it was that we wouldn't be together. I still have that letter with me today. Interestingly, although we weren't technically boyfriend and girlfriend anymore, he called me everyday. I was confused as to why he called me everyday when we weren't a couple. I believe that he didn't want anyone else to have me, so he made sure he was still in the picture and that I wouldn't forget about him. This continued for the next year or so, and we grew to become good friends. I believe that was what God wanted us to be at that time: good friends. God wanted me to see him as a brother in Christ, instead of a boyfriend, and I also believe we both weren't ready for a committed relationship. We had a lot of growing to do in our relationship with God. I thank God for that extra time of being single because I was able to do so much in ministry and learn more about who I was as a leader.

Our relationship became more serious about a year later, when it seemed to finally click and we both believed that God was in it. We dated, but we still didn't spend a lot of time together. Our courtship was mostly over the phone and attending Amway functions with him. One day we started to talk about our relationship and how we believed that this was it for both of us. We weren't looking to date anymore and we knew this would eventually end up in marriage. It's a funny thing, but I felt called to marry him. It's hard to explain this because we didn't have your normal courtship of falling in love, dating, hanging out with our family and friends, and engagement, and then marriage. We still didn't see each other a lot like normal couples, but we just knew that we didn't want to date anymore; we wanted to get married.

He proposed to me at our connect group by putting the engagement ring in my ice cream bowl. I wondered why he kept telling me to eat the ice cream faster. I really didn't want the ice cream because I was lactose intolerant. He didn't know that about me. He got so impatient that he said "Give me that bowl and I'll finish it for you." He started to finish my ice cream and suddenly stopped and said "What is this in your ice cream?" He spit out an engagement ring. He went on his knee and asked me to marry him and I said, "YES!"

We didn't believe in long engagements; because Mike just couldn't keep his hands off of me, like many young Christian couples, we wanted to get married fast. My parents were not that thrilled. They weren't thrilled that I was a Christian, and they weren't thrilled that I was marrying a man with a child, and a man who was not Chinese. They must have been thinking, "What has happened to this child of ours? She becomes a Christian and then she marries a man with a child that is not hers?" This was not the norm for a Chinese family to experience. My parents had hopes and dreams that I would marry a doctor or a rich businessman with lots of money, but instead I wanted to marry a man with a child who worked at the airport and didn't have much money. I still remember telling my parents that we were going to get married, and their response was "no." I felt like a child asking my parents for permission, but I was 26 years old, not 15 years old. I didn't know what to say except that I wanted to marry Mike and be Courtney's mom. I couldn't explain to them what it meant to feel called to marry this man. They wouldn't understand any of it because they weren't believers. Eventually they accepted the conclusion that I was going to marry him and become a mother.

We planned for a great wedding in September and on having a large reception because my parents would not have it any other way. I wanted a cocktail party with appetizers and desserts in the backyard of my pastor's house. That was not going to go well with my parents because it was not appropriate for my Chinese-side of the family. So we had to have a reception with a buffet with three entrées at a hotel because that was the normal way to have a wedding reception. Since they were helping me pay for the wedding, I gave in, and we had the reception at the Outrigger Prince Hotel.

We got married on September 25, 1993, and that was the best day of Mike's life. I mean our life. I finally entered a new chapter in my life with the man I am called to do life with. I often look back at where I was with the boyfriend whom I thought I was going to marry. I am so grateful to God for taking my ex-boyfriend out of my life because I would have settled, and that's not what God wants for His children. He wants to give us the best! So if you're single and wanting to be married, I would highly encourage you not to settle. Make your list of all the characteristics you want in a husband and don't date just to date; date to marry. I've been teaching this to my daughters and all the young ladies that I have the privilege of meeting with. I am very blessed to do life with the man to whom God has called me to be a wife to, and God will call you to a man and be a wife to as well.

While Mike and I were dating, he was in the Amway business. Besides having Jesus in his life, this business really helped to save his life. It taught him leadership, hope, and who he was meant to be – a successful man. He was so beaten down after his divorce from Courtney's mom. God rescued him at the age of twenty-one when life was supposed to have started for him; but instead it was a time of sadness, defeat, and hopelessness. I thank God for his friend, Brandon, who would harass him to go to church with him.

Mike finally did and gave his life to Jesus at Hope Chapel Kaneohe Bay. Friends, church, and the Amway business helped keep him alive.

After we got married, I came alongside to help him with the business. Honestly, I didn't like it that much. I didn't like attending meetings and dressing up. I was watching Mike present the business plan to people and remember thinking that he was really good at communicating. He aspired to be a, "Diamond" in this business that makes millions, and to speak on their platform about how the business has helped him to thousands of people. But something inside of me knew that this was not his calling. Instead of drawing circles and explaining to people how they could be financially independent, I knew his calling was to tell people about Jesus. Maybe that's why I was so resistant to attending all of those meetings and dressing up, because it wasn't what God wanted for Mike. But as a good and supportive wife, I just prayed that he would hear from God and that I would stop being so negative and critical towards the business. I had to step aside and allow God to direct his path. I have to admit, I was trying to be God when I tried to direct Mike's path.

God had been stirring in Mike this calling to become a pastor. He was resisting it big time because he knew that he would have to let go of the Amway business and was afraid of disappointing his friend Brandon and so many others who were in the business with him. Watching him wrestle with this was difficult because so much of his identity was attached to it. He knew what he had to do, but it wasn't going to be easy. He knew he had to obey God.

Mike finally had a meeting with his friend Brandon, and told him what God had been speaking to him about being a pastor full-time and that he needed to exit the business. It was a test of their friendship and that was the hardest thing for Mike. Although his friend wasn't thrilled, Brandon eventually understood and supported him, which was what Mike wanted. Sometimes it will be hard when you obey God. Learning to "let go and let God" is all about complete and total trust. When you learn to trust God with your whole life – and let go of things, relationships, careers, or businesses – you can't help but know that God is in it.

Mike is the man he is today because of his obedience and trust in God. Mike eventually came on staff at Hope Chapel Kaneohe Bay; serving as the pastor in the ministry he called "Honeymooners." This group was for young couples married less than 5 years because he said after that, "the honeymoon is over." After serving in that ministry, he eventually became the youth pastor. He was an amazing youth pastor. He could relate to the kids by sharing all of his wild stories from his youth days living in Honoka'a, Hawai'i, and the kids just loved him. He always said he had the best job in the world being the youth pastor.

Being newly married and a wife and a mother at the same time was not as easy as I thought. I was only 27 when I became an instant mom of a 7 year-old girl. This became the toughest challenge in my life, and it wasn't what I expected it to be.

Chapter Four

Ramen Mom (Instant Mom)

Mike and I were young and newly married with a daughter. When I first met Courtney, she was about 4 years old. She was the cutest little thing. She had a spunky personality, was very talkative, and she loved to dance. She was a beautiful little girl with brown hair, slanted Asian eyes, skinny, and she had a dimple on her left side of her face. She adored her dad. He was everything to her. Her Nana and Papa came to help Mike raise her because it was tough being a single dad at the age of twenty-one. Nana became her mom because her own mom was not present in her life. So, you can imagine, as a young girl without her mom, she had her own struggles that manifested in some of her misbehaviors. I couldn't relate to her pain because my mother had never abandoned me. I'm sure she had questions in her head about my commitment to her and her dad. She wasn't sure of me and she didn't know me, and I felt that it was going to be rough road ahead of us in our mother-daughter relationship as we learned how to trust one another.

I have to be honest, I had no idea how to be a mother. I just did what my mom did for me by replicating that in my own motherhood. Nana instructed me about her morning ritual of having hot chocolate when she wakes up. So I did just that, I made hot chocolate in the morning for her, and made her eggs and Spam. I went all out for breakfast because that's what my mom did for us when were kids. I had to pick her up every day after school, and that was totally new to me. I had been single for a long time, and now I was responsible for another person. There were times when I almost forgot to pick her up from school, and she would often be the last kid picked up. What a bad mom I was, forgetting to pick up her child. I had lots to get accustomed to, but thank God for grace. We were all learning about each other at the same time. I didn't have only my husband's habits, likes, and dislikes to understand; I had two people to figure out. Our first year of marriage was tough for me. I had to blend into this family, and they had to blend into mine. We came from two totally different upbringings – Mike from a Catholic background and myself from a Buddhist background like I mentioned a little earlier. We were raised completely different from how we were disciplined, how we were spoken to, and what we ate. I wasn't used to all of the American food that they ate, and they weren't used to all of the Chinese food that I ate. My parents often liked to eat out for lunch at a dim sum restaurant in Chinatown, and we often ate there weekly with them. Eventually, Mike and Courtney got sick of Chinese food. I remember Mike and Courtney had a difficult time adjusting to my family because they were your typical Chinese family; rude, loud and overbearing. Don't get me wrong, I love my parents, but they were opposite of Mike's parents. My parents spoke more Chinese than English, so Mike and Courtney were often not part of our conversations. My dad would sometimes acknowledge Mike not with a "hello" but with only a nod of his head. That used to really upset Mike, but now he's used to it. As you can imagine, the blending of any two families can be very difficult, especially if one side of the family speaks little English or is used to different mannerisms.

Did I mention this new role of mom and married life took some adjusting to? At the time, Mike was working part-time at American Airlines and in the Amway business. I was working full-time at Hope Chapel Kaneohe Bay, so on the weekends I was busy at church, and Mike and Courtney were enjoying the weekend off with no school or work.

After being married for about three months, I noticed that I was getting a little distant from them because I was having a hard time adjusting to being a wife and an instant mom. The way I dealt with uncomfortable situations was to not engage in the situation or relationship, but to remain silent. I started to shut them out and went about doing my own things. I would often find excuses not to come home once I was finished with work. I would either go to my parents' home or to my sister's home to be with my nephew. I didn't know what to do with my own family. I felt like a nanny at times because all I did was cook, clean, and help Courtney with her homework. There was such a struggle when it came to homework time because Courtney was not easy to work with. I would threaten her, I would ground her, and I would tell her, "Whatever, just get a bad grade on it since you don't want to try." It was so stressful being a parent. I didn't like it. I wasn't used to someone giving me a hard time and giving me attitude. I didn't like the smirk on Courtney's face when she didn't like something that I had made for her to eat. I didn't like having to wake her up in the morning because she wasn't a morning person and was grumpy. This was all new to me! I remember trying to get to know her, so I would take her to the park to go roller blading. We had fun until she got bored or got hurt. Her crying was hard to handle. I didn't know how to comfort her the way she wanted or needed to be comforted. When I got hurt as a child, my parents gave me no sympathy; they said nothing to me and just let me figure it out.

The struggle was real in our family, and I can relate to other blended families. We all come from different upbringings with different styles of parenting and different ways of showing love to one another. When two lives merge together, it's not always a smooth transition, but tend to miss the mark with one another.

One big mark that Mike, Courtney, and I were all missing was how we showed love to one another. Thank God for the book called, *"The Five Love Languages"* by Gary Chapman. This book helped us tremendously with understanding how we wanted to be loved in the five different ways we love which is physical touch, quality time, gift giving, acts of service and encouraging words. We can know each other's love language, but if we don't show or speak their love language, it won't help us in our relationship. We all had to change, especially Mike and I. Mike's love languages are physical touch and encouraging words, and mine are acts of service and quality time. We weren't showing or speaking each other's love languages and that affected our marriage. Courtney's love languages are physical touch and quality time, and physical touch was not my love language at all. I wasn't a hugger or a person who used a lot of encouraging words. When she fell down and got hurt, I didn't know how to comfort her except to tell her that everything was fine and to get back to what she was doing. I didn't kiss her boo boo away or give her a hug; I just spoke to her and thought that would make her feel better. I didn't know what parents do when their kids get hurt. When I got hurt my parents didn't do anything except scold us and tell us that it was our fault. No sympathy was given, no hugs or kisses on our boo boos. Now you can see why we had a difficult first year of marriage and family.

After two years or so, we decided to get some family counseling. It was the best thing for us because our relationship was growing further apart. My marriage was not flourishing, and my relationship with Courtney was growing more complicated. My heart was not in the right place and my love was depleted. We needed help. Every night, I would pray and ask God to forgive me because of how my heart was hardened and bitter. And every morning as I woke up, I would go on my knees and pray and cry out that God would help me that day to love my husband and my daughter. I was a Christian and I needed to act like a Christian; I couldn't be holding on to any bitterness, anger or hurts over them. This was my struggle in the first two years of my marriage. No one said it was going to be easy, but I had no other experience to compare it to. I just had to keep turning to God for His wisdom and help. I couldn't do it without God, and I would not suggest anyone do it without God. I was committed to my marriage, and I held on to God with every muscle and breath that I had.

As we were sitting in the counselor's office, Mike and Courtney were on a couch and I was sitting on a chair, the counselor asked each one of us how we were doing. When it came time for my turn I said, "I don't have any more love to give." I was feeling so depleted that I had nothing left inside of me to offer them. I didn't know how to love anymore or have the tolerance to keep going the way that we were. This was a tough struggle, and we needed a lot of help in understanding one another. Mike felt like he was torn between his daughter and his wife. I felt like it was them against me. I'm not sure how Courtney felt because she was young and wasn't able to articulate her feelings. Her misbehavior was her way of communicating that she didn't like how things were. We were so young and inexperienced with few tools to help us mesh our new family together.

As we sat down with the counselor, she told me that I needed to be more affectionate even if I didn't feel like it. So I asked her, "You mean I have to fake it till I make it?" She said, "YES!" That was so hard for me. I had to do my part in order to save my marriage and our family. So I gave it my best, but it took a long while for things to come around. Mike says that I am much, much better now, but it was one of the biggest battles in our relationship. I needed to show them love in the way that they could receive it, and vice versa. For Mike, he needed to do more cleaning around the house, and I gave him more affection, and of course encouraging words.

It was a tough season of adjusting to becoming a wife and a mother at the same time. I am so glad that season is over, but I am grateful for all of the lessons learned. We all had to change, especially Mike and I. Courtney was still a child and we didn't expect her to change, we just needed to keep her safe and loved. She did go to counseling, and I believe it helped her as she was growing into a young woman. She's an amazing mom now to her daughter, Bowie, and a great wife to her husband, Jaysen. She has become a friend to me, and I love how she and I can communicate with one another with respect and love. She's been through a lot, but having her parents (Mike and I) have a strong marriage helped her to know that we will never leave her and that we will always remain in her life through the good and tough seasons. I believe that one day, she will share or even write a book about her life.

After being married for three years, we had our daughter Rebekah-Taylor in 1996. She's my child who is sweet and very compassionate with a beautiful heart. She was an easy child to raise, but was very attached to me. If ever she had to leave my hips, you would have to peel her away from me as she screamed her lungs out for me to come rescue her. She did ministry with me while I pushed her around the church in a stroller each weekend. She was also a thumb sucker, and that thumb was always in her mouth with two fingers touching her eyebrows, similar to how you would hold a bowling ball. She is very athletic like her mom. Yeah Right! She is athletic like her dad, of course. She played soccer, basketball, and volleyball. Her love was volleyball, and she played club ball all her teen life and now plays in college as well.

When Rebekah was three years old, we decided to try and have another child. It was a tough season of trying and would eventually take us six years to have another child. I had prayed and knew that God said we would have another one, but six years, Lord? We tried many different types of procedures to try to get pregnant, but none worked. I can truly empathize when a couple is having a hard time conceiving and can relate to their frustration, guilt, condemnation, and having to be disappointed each month. It was a tough season for me because I couldn't understand why I couldn't get pregnant when we hadn't had a difficult time conceiving Rebekah. It was tough being happy for other women who got pregnant when I wanted so badly to have another child. It actually consumed me for six years and felt like I was almost addicted to the process of trying each month. My only peace was that God said that I would have another child, and I clung to that promise. Others had a word for me as well while believing with me, saying, "It's coming, just wait patiently." That was the only hope that I had left: His Word.

If you're dealing with this right now, my prayer for you is that you find peace and hope in God through it all. Don't put guilt or shame on yourself because of any past mistakes that you may have made with your body. Take this season as a season of growing to trust God and knowing that God is God; He never changes and His love endures forever. God is the maker of all life, and He destined each life in His own timing. You and I can try and do all we know in the natural, but at the end of all this, it's still God's design and God's timing. You just have to leave it to Him. I know it's not easy, but He is the giver of life. Hang in there and make sure you enjoy this season with your husband and your other children, if you have them. I have had the privilege of praying over many women, and I have to say that 50% of them got pregnant. I truly believe that if you're a woman who has had children, you should pray for the women who desire to have one of their own. Don't give up believing; just keep your eyes on Jesus. When that baby comes, know that I'm celebrating with you, and make sure you bring that baby to Hawai'i!

Eventually, I did get pregnant, and it was in the month that I said to God that I was completely done trying. I was having one of those moments when I just threw in the towel and gave up. But I was at peace about not having to try anymore because I was content with my two girls. So, when I was late that month with my period, I didn't want to get my hopes up high because I had done that before and was disappointed. I didn't want to pick up a pregnancy test because I'm so "Chinese" (frugal), that I didn't want to waste a kit. I waited until I was two weeks late, and that's when I actually told Mike that I may be pregnant. I called for a doctor's appointment, and you know how it is when you're waiting for the doctor to come back to the room to tell you if you're pregnant or not. I held my breath as he entered the room and smiled and said, "You are PREGNANT!" I couldn't believe that he said I was pregnant! I called Mike and we were so thankful that it had finally come, so thankful that God had given us another child. He gave us another girl, and her name is Charis. She came into the world in 2005. Our family was now complete.

Charis is our Chinese firecracker princess. I remember looking into her eyes as I first held her in my arms, and she just wouldn't stay focused. She kept looking around with curiosity, as if she had to know everything that was happening. I opened her up from her swaddle and wanted to see every part of her tiny body. She was a petite one, but as I looked at her hands and feet, I noticed how big her feet were. I thought, "What did I eat that made her feet so big?" I put her feet to my hands to see how big they were, and they were thin and big. I told Mike that I think she will be our tallest one. She's amazingly beautiful and smart. She's the youngest and the baby of the family, and we all adore her. She has a strong personality and knows what she wants and when she wants it. She loves watching, The Fixer-Upper show and Cupcake Wars. She will be our home designer and baker one day, but we have also been sowing seeds that one day she will be the pastor of this church, and we will see her preaching all over the world.

Interestingly, my girls are nine years apart, and each child represents a different season in our lives as we look back. We have seen what God has done in our lives in each season, and how He merged our two lives together to have the life we have today. We are truly blessed with what God has given us. Three beautiful girls and a beautiful granddaughter, Bowie, and an amazing son-in-law, Jaysen. Our life is rich and full.

I still remember that prayer on the day of my salvation, "Lord, change me and give me a new life." I did not expect the life that I have today. It's amazing and so fruitful!

As Mike and I served on staff at Hope Chapel Kaneohe Bay with our two girls, Mike became the youth pastor and I was leading the children's ministry. We were both content in the ministries we were leading and believed we were going to work there forever. Mike would sometimes preach for our senior pastor and that really helped him with his communication gift, as well as being under one of the best bible teachers on this island. Our two girls were thriving in the church and building strong friendships and were involved with missions and helping in the children's ministry. But God had a different plan for us.

CHAPTER FIVE

CONTENT IN MINISTRY AND GROWING AS A COUPLE

Life was good at HCKB because I grew so much spiritually as a leader and as a wife and mother. We did life with the people at church, as well as with our senior pastors, Ralph and Ruby Moore. Ralph and Ruby took us under their wings and became such great mentors. Mike learned how to change the oil in our cars, as well as how to invest our money. If it wasn't for Ralph's wisdom, we wouldn't have bought our first home. Mike and Ralph spent a lot of time at McDonald's just talking about life and ministry. I met with Ruby every so often, and she would share with me about what it is to be the wife of a senior pastor and how to run a children's ministry. Courtney and Rebekah learned how to swim in their pool, and we often had meals at their home. I love Ruby's angel eggs (deviled eggs), and we called them that because we never wanted to give the devil any credit for those delicious eggs. Lots of great memories were built there in their home. We were so blessed to be under the leadership of Pastors Ralph and Ruby Moore, and because they allowed us to be a part of their family.

We all need people like that in our lives; people who will invest their wisdom and time to help us, especially young couples in the beginning seasons of their married lives. Because of their example, we carry that same culture with the people in our church. We love the people that God has blessed us with, and we take seriously our responsibility as senior pastors to shepherd these people well and with integrity. When Mike and I decided to accept the position of senior pastors of a large church community on the west side of Oahu, we said we would do our best and lead well. We knew we were discipled well by our pastors, and were very well equipped to pastor a church. Our pastor, Ralph, is known for planting churches, and under his leadership of Hope Chapel, over 700 churches have been planted all over the world.

Mike and I were content in our positions as the children's and youth pastors. We had amazing teams under us, and the ministries were thriving. We both had never thought of leaving our parent church or ever starting our own church. There was one time that Mike had thought of maybe planting a church in Oregon. It didn't go well when he mentioned it to me. In my spirit I didn't think he was ready to be a senior pastor, and Oregon was not really a place that I wanted to live. He chose Oregon because his sister and brother lived there, and so did his parents, who had moved to Oregon after Mike and I were married to start a new venture. I remember telling Pastor Ralph about Mike's idea and told him that I believed Mike was not ready. "Please, don't send us," I said. He also agreed that Mike was not ready to plant a church. My husband is such a visionary and loves to dream big and live big. He used to scare me a lot with his visions and dreams. I'm a consistent, mellow, and structured type of person, and of course I married the opposite. But that is what I love about my husband; he makes my world insane, spontaneous, fun, and busy. He is showing me the world, literally! I always feel like *Princess Jasmine* who met the beggar boy *Ali* from the movie *Aladdin*.

Mike and I worked well together in ministry with him running the youth and me the children's ministry. We literally had all of the youth under our leadership. There was a season when Mike had just came on staff and I had been working full-time for about three years. I had a senior position on staff and he was a support staff member. I knew it was a little uncomfortable for him because I was his wife and also a senior leader over him. We definitely had to understand our roles as husband and wife, and then as peers at work. Mike and I were the first married couple to work on staff together, and we didn't know if it was going to work out or not. Thank God it did, but there were times when it wasn't easy for me.

As a wife and a mother and a leader in the church, I had to learn how to balance my life. Many women ask me the question, "How do you and Mike do ministry together with young children?" First of all, you have to know what your gifts are. Not all of us are called to lead, teach, or pastor. Some of us are called to be servants, intercessors, or administrators. All gifts work together for the body of Christ. Once you know and understand how to use your gifts, you operate in them. I had the gifts of leadership, administration, and wisdom and Mike had the gifts of pastor, leadership, teacher, and evangelist. We both wanted each other to succeed, and we both wanted to do our best in doing what God had called us to do. Mike was growing as a leader and a preacher and had other responsibilities in the church. We both just had to learn how to manage our time and calendars.

God made women so differently from men. Women can think about five things or more at a single time, juggle them all and make them work. I knew the schedules of my girls, my husband, and the church. I had to manage it all and make it work for everyone. I believe that when God calls a couple to be married, he is joining two people with different gifts, as well as talents, and meshing them into one. We both can accomplish great things for the Lord individually, but together it's even better. I always had to remind myself that I am the wife and I am under my husband's authority, and he watches over my life and makes sure that I am healthy and the kids are doing well. I always made sure to have a calendar and to be mindful of his schedule and the kids' schedules. We over communicated because we needed to be clear on our expectations and to have a balance. The children have always done ministry with us. My girls helped in the classroom with the little kids and also helped at the different events we had. I wanted our family to do life and ministry together. They never complained because they had friends at church, and they loved coming to church. My daughter, Rebekah, had a best friend named Tiana, and they were like two peas in a pod. You would see them everywhere on the campus; in the sanctuary, the office, or in the classroom, just goofing off and having fun with some of our leaders. They spent a lot of time together on the weekends and after school playing, doing their homework, and joking around. Great memories were made for my kids and the other kids whose parents were also on staff.

If you are dating or married to a person who is in ministry, it can be very rewarding to do ministry together. Both callings are important, and we need to honor one another's gifts and be the best cheerleaders for one another. If you're single and dating someone, make sure you understand that person's calling and gifting. If the person you are dating is called to do missions and you're not, please rethink that relationship. If the person is called to pastor a church, then make sure you are on-board because you will be sharing him with so many people, and you have to be okay with that. Understanding each others' calling and gifting is so important because it can either make your marriage great, or the church or ministry can become a mistress. Take care of your family first and make ministry secondary to your family. You can have it all – family and ministry – you just need to manage it well. And don't just manage the calendar, but manage your heart. Don't ever let your heart become bitter or jealous towards your spouse's calling or gifting. Remember, the two shall become one! His rewards are your rewards. Your rewards are his rewards. His success is your success, and your success is his success. Don't compare one another; be for each other and be the best encourager. Like I said, doing ministry together as a husband and wife can work, and it benefits the church and will benefit your family.

Both of our ministries were flourishing, we were growing as senior leaders in the church, and life was good. I had been overseeing the children's ministry for about ten years, and I'll be honest, I was getting bored with my job. It was easy, and the ministry was running well with the leaders and teachers that I had in place. I felt like I had no more vision for the ministry and I asked myself this question, "What am I supposed to do next?" This was also at the time that we had been trying to have another baby and it wasn't working. We weren't getting pregnant, and I couldn't see myself running the children's ministry forever. I had a plan in my head; I thought that when I got pregnant that would be when I quit my job. That would be the best excuse to use instead of just quitting with no reason at all. But that didn't happen. Instead, a church plant was being offered to us by our senior pastor. The offer came out of nowhere. We were completely stunned that our pastor would ask us and in awe of such an honor.

CHAPTER SIX

A NEW CHURCH AND ASSIGNMENT

Our pastor asked us to visit a church called Hope Chapel Waikele, on the west side of Oahu, whose senior pastor had decided to step down. The church had plateaued at about sixty people, and for some reason, I felt in my spirit that this was the right time for Mike to become the senior pastor of a church. I had a good feeling about this, but it would bring about a big change to our lives. We had just bought our first home a couple of years prior that was close in proximity to our current church, and taking over this Waikele church would require a 30-45 minute drive to the west side. Where you're from you may not think that is a far drive, but that's the way we see it here in Hawai'i. Anytime you have to drive more than 30 minutes, we consider that a long drive. I didn't want to move out of my new house to the other side of the island. In addition to that, the church held services in a hot, elementary school cafeteria that had no air conditioning. I was constantly hot in that place, and it was going to be terrible for my hair! I remember those early days of doing church when we had to set up and break down each weekend. I guess I was getting too comfortable at a permanent facility, and it was time for us to get out of our complacency and have new vision for our ministry and life.

We went that Sunday to visit the church, but we didn't tell the senior pastor of Hope Chapel Waikele that we were coming, although he and Mike first met each other two weekends prior to our visit. Ironically, they had never met before, even though we were a part of the same church movement on the same island. Our pastor suggested we check it out and get a feel for the place, so we showed up like new visitors, and yes, the church had one service at 10:00am and was very small. The church service was pretty basic. They were doing the best they could with what they had, and the people were nice and demographically a little bit older than expected. We did like the school facility because it was one of the newer schools, so it didn't look as rundown as some of the other schools in Hawai'i. It was a fairly new community, as the west side of Oahu was booming with new homes and a lot of young families. There was a lot of potential on the west side, and it was a great opportunity for the church to grow, and we saw that it had a lot of potential. We went away that day and said that we would commit to praying about this.

Mike and I went away to Waikiki and spent a couple of nights of fasting and just praying and talking about it. In fact, we were blessed by a couple in our church, Karen and Doug, with a complimentary two-night stay at the Double Tree Hotel. On the last day of our stay, we looked at each other and both agreed that this was something God wanted us to do. We were apprehensive because we didn't know if we could lead a church, but God showed me a picture of Moses walking down from Mt. Sinai carrying the Ten Commandments, and the glory of the Lord was on him and apparent to all because he had encountered God. As I was looking at Mike's hair, I noticed that he was getting just a little gray, and that was the sign that God gave me that he was ready to be the senior pastor of a church. There was more to it than that, but at that moment when Mike and I prayed, that's what was impressed upon me.

We went back to our pastor and told him that we had prayed about it and would accept the Lord's call to lead the church. Our pastor said he needed Mike there in two weeks, and that was definitely a shocker! Two weeks! We didn't have a team, and we didn't know how to re-start this church. Plus, Mike still had to run the youth ministry until his replacement arrived in about 3 months. His replacement was our pastor's son, Carl Moore. Mike had to work a dual role as the senior pastor of Hope Chapel Waikele, do his best to build a team and create momentum to turn the church around, and continue to lead the youth ministry until Carl arrived. Our pastor was gracious enough to allow me to stay on board in my current role for another two years until Mike could get established. This was a huge blessing because otherwise, I'm not sure what we would have had to do to replace my salary if I had to resign my position, but God had it all worked out for us.

So in 2001, the Lord called Mike and I to re-plant the church and change the name to Hope Chapel West O'ahu (HCWO). I believe God had been preparing us for this from the first day we were planted at Hope Chapel Kaneohe Bay, being discipled by our own senior pastor. We came from a church family that has the culture of planting churches as a form of evangelism. There are over 700 churches with the name Hope Chapel, and our pastor has been so instrumental in many of those church plants. Mike and I were very blessed to have been under his leadership. He was like a father to me from the first day I attended the church, when I had a broken heart. He would always make a point of talking with me after service to see how I was doing or if I had any questions about the message. He took an interest in my spiritual walk and helped me through my breakup. He was the one who saw leadership potential in me, and if he had never asked me to be a part of the team, I'm not sure where I would be. So thank you, Pastor Ralph and Ruby. I am so blessed by your love and for having faith in me.

The day the Lord sent us out to start Hope Chapel West O'ahu, God knew the plan He had for us, but we didn't know how big it was. As I shared in my previous chapters, I was not a part of the team that helped establish the first two years of the church because I was working at Hope Chapel Kaneohe Bay. It was taking a toll on each of us and on our marriage because I wasn't growing with Mike or with the church. I would go to the events and attend services, but would have to leave and head back to work and finish my day there. After one summer of running a VBS (Vacation Bible School) at HCKB, I became so exhausted and it felt as if I was attending both churches; doing everything for each one, so much so that I grew tired and weary. That was a turning point in my life when I knew that we had to make a decision, but it was hard because of our finances. Mike finally made the decision for me and said, "You are going to quit." So I told Mike that he needed to tell Ralph because I didn't want to disappoint him. Ralph believed that we could work like this, but our church was growing and Mike really wanted me to do what I was doing at HCKB, at our own church. He felt that I was giving all of my talents and gifts to HCKB and not to HCWO. So, I finally told Ralph; he wasn't happy, but he understood. I felt as if this burden lifted off of me, and I believed that this was an opportunity for another person to have my job. I was very blessed to have led the children's ministry because I was able to lead so many wonderful people and see so many children's lives changed. I believe that if you have a fun, bible-based teaching and fun-loving teachers, kids will want to come to church and parents will want to come as well. Children's ministry is a vital ministry for the church because it brings families and communities to church. In fact, our good friend, consultant and author Dr. Sam Chand, refers to children's ministry as the "engine room" of the church. No one wants to attend a church with a boring children's ministry. So, thank you to all those servants who serve so faithfully in the children's and youth ministries. My hats off to you!!!

I was finally attending only one church, and it was our church. It felt good to be at just one church and be able to be planted and rooted. I intentionally made every effort to greet and get to know the people. Strangely but understandably, many of the members had no idea who I was in the beginning because I wasn't visible in the first two years. In his sermons, Mike kept referring to his wife Lisa, but most didn't know who this Lisa really was until I got more involved. I was so happy to be with him, finally leading at the same place with the same purpose.

I had a hard time adjusting to my role as a senior pastor's wife; even though I had been the wife of a pastor for a long time, being the wife of a senior pastor who had the responsibility of leading a church was definitely new for me. After leaving the staff at HCKB, I came on staff part-time at HCWO and was now, finally part of the team. Week after week, just sitting and learning about our church gave me such an appreciation for my husband's leadership. I was so proud of him and what he had accomplished since starting the church. He was the perfect person to lead this body, and I was watching him grow; becoming such an influential leader and pastor. I thought, "Who is this guy?" One of the biggest transitions for me was seeing my husband as my pastor. Yes, he was my pastor. Pastor Ralph had always been my pastor, and now God was saying to me that Mike was my pastor and that I would learn and grow under his leadership and influence. It was very humbling for me. That is what you call submission! Not only did I have to submit to him at home, but at church as well. Mike sure loved it when I told him this. Listening to him week after week really helped me to grow into my next season. I enjoyed listening to him and really believed that he was one of the best communicators on the island. I was in awe, and I was even more in awe knowing that he was my husband and I was his wife. I was a very proud wife.

Our youngest daughter, Charis (pronounced Ka-riss), came into the world in 2005, and this was her church. She never knew anything about HCKB except from the stories she heard or the people she met. I have been so blessed to be able to stay home and be a mom and a pastor with both Rebekah and Charis. The greatest joy of my life was to be able to raise my children and not have to send them off to a sitter. I know many moms do that and I know it's not easy when you have to drop them off. I remember praying about whether to be a stay-at-home mom or go back to work after I had Rebekah. Strangely, I felt I was supposed to go back to work. I struggled with that because I wanted to do both. I wanted to stay at home with Rebekah and continue ministry full-time. I remember asking my boss, Pastor Ralph, if I could work part-time and he had said, "No." He said, "It's either full-time or nothing at all." I was shocked when he said that, but then he said, "What if you work from home, full-time?" I looked at him and said, "Really? Could I?" and he said, "Yes." That was the best thing that ever happened to me, to have both and not have to give up one for the other. I thank God for that decision, and I made sure that I worked hard at home and made every day count. I went in for staff meetings while my mom watched her for us, and then headed back home to work and care for her. I was the staff member on weekends with the baby in the stroller, walking from classroom to classroom on campus, making sure things were running smoothly for the ministry. Rebekah literally grew up around children's ministry. The great thing was that once she was of age to attend preschool and kindergarten, my life regained some normalcy and I went back to the office for work. I also had the privilege of being a stay-at-home mom while working at home when Charis was born. I am truly blessed to have had the opportunity to raise my girls and watch them grow.

The church (HCWO) was growing, and the cafeteria filled up each weekend to the point that we didn't have any chairs left to set up. We were spilling over into the courtyard and parking became a problem. It was a good thing and a great problem to have. Our church could not contain the growth, and we had to look for another place. Mike had his eye on a vacant furniture store at the Waikele Shopping Center. He told me as we drove by each weekend that it was going to be our church. I didn't believe him and thought that he was shooting for the moon on that one. I thought that there was no way we could afford that place, but he often would tell me "All things are possible with God, if you believe." And I didn't believe it would happen. For about two to three years, he confessed and prophesied over the vacant space, making several approaches to the owners of the shopping center, but received no response. Even though Mike was rejected many times, he didn't stop pursuing. He wouldn't settle and was persistent. Thank God for that because we ended up getting that space after several years of asking.

I loved pastoring our church because of the many faithful and loving people that called Hope Chapel West O'ahu home. Within a year and a half after moving into the shopping center, our church doubled in attendance. We have this saying that people were waiting for us to occupy that warehouse and once we did, they decided to come. The faith of the people and the faith of our pastor is what got us this place. It sure wasn't my faith, as I did repent for my lack of faith. I learned a big lesson at that time; never underestimate the power of God and what He can do for His children, and never underestimate your husband!

Charis was now about four years old, and we were in the new facility and the church was growing rapidly – life was good! Charis would be attending pre-school full-time, and I was definitely ready. While she was at school five days a week, I was working at home and taking care of the house, when something inside of me started feeling unsettled. I was actually getting bored in what I was doing at church, leading overseers of ministries, and I came to a place in my life where I had questions lingering in my mind. Is there more to life than this, than being a mom and a ministry overseer? Am I meant to do more? Am I making an impact with the gifts and talents that God gave me? I wanted something more to do, but I didn't know what it was. I still remember praying and asking God these questions, but little did I know that God was preparing me for something more than I could ever have expected.

PART TWO

AWAKENED

CHAPTER SEVEN

A NEW SEASON COMES

14 *for the light makes everything visible. This is why it is said, "Awake, O sleeper, rise up from the dead, and Christ will give you light."* **Ephesians 5:14 (NLT)**

We hosted our first conference called "The HNL Conference". It was Mike's idea at the time, but it didn't really fit. But nobody wanted to tell him. HNL is the abbreviation used for Honolulu International Airport. Mike had attended his very first Hill song Conference in Sydney, Australia, and one of the speakers was Pastor Ed Young from Fellowship Church in Dallas, Texas. He kept saying, "We are going to an HNL, a 'Ho notha level!'" and Mike kept repeating it. So, he decided to call the conference the HNL Conference because of course, he had every intention to go to a whole 'nother level. Who could argue with that? It was our second equipping conference because we wanted to equip our leaders and invite other pastors from the island to come and join us. I believe there were about 300 people in attendance with local pastors like Norman Nakanishi of Grace Bible Church, Dave Barr of New Hope Windward, Art and Kuna Sepulveda of Word of Life, and our very own Mike Kai serving as the main speakers. We had learned how to host conferences from attending conferences in Australia and Kona. Mike is a learner, and he wanted to learn from the best, so he sought out people whose churches were growing because he wanted to learn how to grow our church. I remember he attended those outside conferences without me because Charis was young and Rebekah had a busy life with school and club volleyball. One summer while he was attending the Hillsong Conference by himself, he told me that I needed to go with him the following year because he wanted me to see what he had been seeing. I was hesitant because Charis was still a young baby, but said that I'd go with him the next time that he went to the conference.

The following summer I went to the Hillsong Conference and was blown away at how huge it was. There were so many people in that arena, it was overwhelming. I come from a small island, so this felt so big. I also had to stay with Charis in her classroom because that's how the conference ran childcare for children under the age of three. I really thought it was a waste of money for me to be there because all I did was sit in a classroom filled with two and three year olds and their moms, and watch the conference on a monitor. I had a bad attitude, and it was freezing in Australia. It was our summer and it was their winter. I wasn't used to the weather and I felt sorry for Charis because her nose was so red. I wasn't happy, and Mike knew it. He encouraged me to sit in the conference while he stayed with Charis. I remember walking in the arena and sitting on the bottom floor and looking around to see 15,000 people. I tried to stay focused on the speaker, but I just couldn't because I was overwhelmed by the people, the screens, and the massiveness of the conference. I can't even tell you if I received anything that was said or if God spoke to me. I came back to Mike and he asked, "What did you think?" I didn't have much to say, I told him I was overwhelmed and that it was okay. I know that's not what he wanted to hear from me, but I had given it a try.

As I shared in the last chapter, Charis had started school and at the same time, I felt this discontentment that I wanted and needed to do more. We were now heading into our second HNL conference, and this time we had our first guest speaker from outside of Hawai'i, named John Bevere. Mike had met him at a conference and read several of his books and held him in high regard. When John said yes to Mike's invitation to speak at our church and conference, Mike was thrilled, like a kid who just scored a touchdown in a football game. I really didn't know who John was because I hadn't read his books or ever heard about him for that matter.

The team worked hard planning for this conference that was to be held in February 2009. Many of the people knew of John Bevere, so we had a larger number of people attending this conference than the previous year, and we were finally in our newly renovated sanctuary, which looked amazing. The day of the conference, I walked into my office and heard that John was in the green room (a room which looked like a living room and not literally a green room). I was a little nervous to meet him because I wasn't sure exactly what I would say. I felt intimidated by his popularity and was sure that he was very knowledgeable about the bible. I was actually afraid that he was going to ask me questions about the bible that I couldn't answer. I finally went into the room and introduced myself to him. I still remember him asking me, "Is it Mrs. Kai or Pastor Lisa?" I'm like, "Just Lisa." I still had a hard time with people calling me Pastor Lisa. I had a pastor's license, but to be called "Pastor" was very uncomfortable for me. We didn't have a culture of honor yet in our church, and John would teach us a lot about the subject in his book, "*Honor's Reward.*" John and I chatted a little, but I couldn't wait to get out of the room because I didn't want him to know that I felt intimidated by him. I wanted to be cool, as if I had it all together. I'm not sure what "having it all together" looked like, but I didn't want him to know that I was very nervous with him.

During worship on the first night of conference, I watched John as he danced and worshiped. It wasn't normal to see a pastor not just standing there with his hands raised, but dancing and moving around and getting into the worship. He was surely different from any other pastors I've known. He went onstage and shared his first message on "Having an Extraordinary Life." I was blown away by his message because it was a message on God's grace and I have never heard of grace spoken in such a way. He said God's grace gives us the ability to go beyond our ability, and God empowers us to serve God acceptably. As he spoke, I experienced something I had never experienced before while sitting and listening to someone preach. Something inside of me woke up! I literally felt a shift happening inside my spirit. I felt a fire inside of me that wanted to burst out and say, "I WANT THAT EXTRAORDINARY LIFE!" In our church when someone said something good as they preached, we didn't respond with an amen, yes, or hallelujah. We were an unresponsive church at the time, or should I say a quiet and respectful church that reflected our humility as people of Hawai'i. John was loud, and we weren't used to that kind of preaching, but I actually liked it. I heard things more clearly, and I was so moved by the Spirit that I wanted to respond, but it's wasn't normal for the pastor's wife to be out of her element – quiet, poised, sitting by her husband in the front, and wearing clothes that didn't show any skin. I'm not trying to put anyone down, but from the examples I've seen in my life, that's what I thought I had to be. I was trying to put myself in a box, but I wanted to get out of that box; I just didn't know how or where to turn. After John spoke and came offstage, I couldn't look at him because I thought that he would know that something had happened inside of me. I didn't want him to ask me any questions, so I avoided him. I think if he had asked me anything, I probably would have started to cry, and I didn't want that.

The next night, John preached again, this time on "Overcoming Intimidation." It really hit home and literally was a slap in my face. As he was speaking, I heard truths that I'd never heard, and these truths were piercing through the marrow of my bones. I felt like I was on fire, which I know now was the Holy Spirit's presence upon me. After his message he called us to do something that I thought I would never do. He asked if anyone wanted to overcome intimidation, and if so, to stand to your feet. The next thing I knew, without thinking, I shot up out of my seat and raised my hand high. I didn't care if anyone looked at me or saw me, the pastor's wife, standing up. I didn't care if anyone thought that I had a problem with intimidation. I just knew I had to overcome it. Hey, I was intimidated by John when I walked into the green room, so it was clearly present in my life. I wanted to get rid of it, and I wanted to be released of it.

After we stood up, he made us shout out loud, really loud, from the depths of our being. It was so weird, but every one of us that stood up – which was almost the entire congregation – started shouting from with everything within them! It was a roar that was louder than anything I had heard at a football stadium or basketball arena! It was so freeing, and so much healing took place that night. We all came away having done something that we had never done in our lives, and it was refreshing. We came out of our shells like a turtle that finally stuck its neck out to see what's around him.

The conference ended, and we took John and another guest speaker, Ben Houston from Hillsong Church in Australia, to lunch. Mike and Ben had struck a friendship while in Sydney. Typical Mike, always making friends. We had Charis with us, and I have to say, I still felt a little intimidated by John and really didn't want to have any conversations, so I used being preoccupied with Charis as an excuse to avoid having to talk to him. I was so glad Mike was there because I relied on him a lot to be my protector when it came to having uncomfortable conversations or being in an environment where I felt intimidated. John sat across from me though, and I said to myself, "Oh boy, how will I try to avoid conversation with the anointed one?" So I mustered enough courage to ask him about his wife, whom I did not know anything about. At this time I was still overseeing ministry leaders, and one of the leaders of the women's ministry was stepping down, so I needed to find a replacement for her. For a season, we had two ladies who oversaw the ministry, and they felt like they weren't supposed to lead it anymore, but would continue to do so until a replacement was found. Mike and I had a conversation about having a women's conference instead of a women's retreat because we felt that we'd be able to reach more people at a conference than at a retreat. As I was conversing with John, I asked him if his wife would speak at our conference, if we decided to have one. He looked at me and didn't give me an answer, but asked me if I had ever attended the Colour Conference in Australia. *The Colour Conference* is a massive women's conference hosted by Hillsong Church. I told John I had never attended that conference because I wasn't "into" women's conferences for the most part. He highly suggested I attend the conference, which was only three weeks away, and that his wife Lisa would be there because she never misses this conference. Ben, who is the son of the senior pastors Brian and Bobbie Houston, was sitting right next to John and said that the conference was sold out but that he could get me in. I made the excuse that it was just too late for me to find airfare that would be cheap enough for us to afford, plus Mike and I would be coming back that week from a vacation that we had been planning to Argentina. We would be heading back on a Tuesday, and the conference started on that Thursday. In order for me to attend this conference, I would be flying in on Tuesday and getting right back on a plane the next morning. I just couldn't see that happening and felt that going was out of the question. I really didn't want to miss seeing my daughters longer than the planned vacation, but they were also a good excuse for why I couldn't attend. I tried to change the subject because I was getting a little uncomfortable, plus John never answered my question if Lisa would speak at a women's conference for us.

That night we had a dinner with some guests from out of town that had attended our conference. I shared with some friends my experience at the conference and how great it was, as well as my conversation with John earlier at lunch. We laughed about it because I said there was no way I could come back from the Argentina trip and get on another plane to Australia. After talking with those friends, a couple, who were Mike's good friends from American Airlines, started to share with me that God had put me on his heart before our conference, and that he felt compelled to tell me that God will be doing something great in my life and that I must get ready. My friends and I looked at each other, and something inside of me said, "I think I am supposed to go to this conference." My friends also agreed that I was to attend this conference, but I felt very flustered and bothered by this whole experience. God was definitely making it clear that I must attend this women's conference in Australia.

The next day, I started to look into flights, and we found a flight that would have me arriving just in time for the opening of the conference. Mike called Ben and asked him if he could help me get a hotel room and register me for the conference. I was so scared because I had never traveled alone to another country; this was new to me. I couldn't believe I was going to do this. I was worried about how I would get to the conference and to the hotel. But all of that was taken care of by Ben, and that's when I really knew that this had to be all God. God was going to show me something, and in order for me to see it and to hear from God, I had to be at this conference.

We had a great time in Argentina and it was an amazing country. It was one of Mike's dreams as a young child to visit Argentina because of a song he had heard over and over again when he was visiting family in the Philippines for a month. It was from Andrew Lloyd Webber's play *Evita* and the song was *Don't Cry for Me Argentina*. He recalls telling his mom, "One day, I'm going to go to Argentina and find out why this woman told people to stop crying for her." Twenty-something years later, Mike stayed true to his word, booked the flights with miles scrounged up from who knows where, and before I could say "no," it was a done deal. I came home, and I had missed my girls so much and I thought to myself, "How am I going to do this? How am I going to leave on another trip?" I had to make sure Mike could handle the girls all by himself, with the cooking, the taking them to school, and the homework. I didn't have any time to prepare for the upcoming week that I would be gone. I had to just trust that Mike would be fine with the girls, and that the girls would be fine with him. In fact, it was Mike who really urged me to go. He promised he would handle it all.

I was all packed and ready to go. I had my journal and a book that I wanted to read on the airplane, *Out of Control and Loving It* by Lisa Bevere. My girlfriend Joan had loaned me the book and said it was one of the best book she's read and that I should read it. Since I didn't know much about Lisa, I thought I would read her book before I met her. I was on the plane all by myself; sitting way in the back, I opened the book and started to read and couldn't put it down. Everything she said in that book described me and what I was going through and how I was feeling. I took so many notes in my journal; I cried, laughed, and cried again. Her story resonated with my life, and I loved how she communicated with such rawness and such humor. I started to like this woman without even having met her. I read her prayers at the end of each chapter, and I felt like she was praying for me. A thought came to my head after reading her book; I felt God tell me that she would be a mentor in my life. I thought, "You're kidding, God, there's no way she would mentor me." I laughed it off and didn't think much about it after that.

I couldn't believe how God was speaking to me through our conference a month ago, to my lunch with John and the invitation to attend the Colour Conference, to reading Lisa's book. It was all God's timing, since the time I had prayed that God would show me what my next season would look like. I really believed that God wanted me to see something, so He could tell me something about my future. On that ten and a half hour flight to Sydney, I could not sleep. I just read the whole book and wrote down everything that I felt the Lord was showing me. I was ready, and was anticipating all that God had for me in Sydney, Australia.

CHAPTER EIGHT

SPOKEN INTO THE ATMOSPHERE

I landed in Sydney, got my luggage, exited out of customs, and someone had a sign that read, "Lisa Kai." Wow, that was the first time that someone ever had a sign for me as I walked out of customs or at any airport, and I felt really important. *That Ben Houston must have some major influence*, I thought. The driver got me to the conference just in the nick of time as the conference opener began. What was so impressive was they had a reserved seat for me. Now that is what you call excellent service. God really set me up well!

I sat next to my friend, Sarah, who used to work for Hillsong Church, but had just moved back to Hawai'i with her husband and kids. I felt more comfortable sitting next to someone that I knew. As I looked around the arena, I noticed there were thousands of women at this conference. I was looking for Lisa Bevere, and I spotted her a couple of rows down from me. I recognized her face from the back of her book. The opener was beautiful, and the worship was so great. The first speaker was Bobbie Houston, who is the pastor of Hillsong Church and the host of the conference. I listened intently to her message, and the Lord was definitely preparing my heart. As the first night was ending, I noticed Lisa was getting ready to leave, and I mustered enough courage to go up to her and introduce myself. I said "Hi, I'm Lisa Kai from Hawai'i, and your husband John was at my church for a conference." And she said, "Yes, John told me about you, and I'm so glad you're here." I felt very comfortable meeting her, as if we knew one another from a long time ago. Lisa made me feel so special because she said that she was looking out for me because John wanted her to meet me. Part of me felt like I was one of those many people that she meets every day, and she probably wouldn't remember me again.

The driver drove me to the hotel, and I checked in to my room. It was weird being in a hotel room alone. I didn't know what to do with myself and I wasn't used to the quiet, so I turned on the television and locked the door. In fact, I put a chair by the door, just in case someone tried to come into my room unannounced. I couldn't call Mike because it was very late due to the time difference, so I had to wait until the next day to call him. I showered and began to pray and journal about the night. I didn't quite see or hear anything specific yet, so I anxiously waited for the next day of the conference.

I woke up, and the drivers were ready to take the ladies from the hotel to the conference. I sat in the shuttle and pretty much kept to myself. I felt so awkward because I didn't know anyone there. I couldn't really share what was happening inside of me, and how this whole adventure of coming to this conference was a

God thing. I felt like I was high on drugs, but without the drugs. I can't explain the feeling, but I just know that God's presence had been very evident in my life for the several months leading up to this week.

I walked to my reserved seat and waited for the conference to begin. All of the other ladies were chatting with one another, as if they'd known each other forever. I just sat and kept to myself until Sarah came to her seat. Worship began, and I recognized one of the songs they were singing, and it was speaking to my heart and spirit. It was a song called *"Awakening."* The lyrics resonated deep inside of me and translated and expressed what I'd been feeling over the past several months:

> For You and You alone
> Awake my soul, awake my soul and sing
> For the world You love
> Your will be done, let Your will be done in me

> Like the rising sun that shines
> From the darkness comes a light
> I hear Your voice and this is my
> Awakening

Something was awakened inside of me while worshiping to this song. This was the same feeling that I had since our conference, and I couldn't shake it off. It was like something completely shifted inside of me, and I wasn't the same person. Something had awakened, and honestly, I had never felt so alive since the day of my salvation. I couldn't put it into words, but God was definitely making a shift in my life and He was calling me. Like I said, I heard a trumpet sound years ago and I didn't know what it meant, but I was now beginning to understand that God was trying to get my attention, and He wanted to put these women, Lisa Bevere and Bobbie Houston, in my life. God wanted me to see something that they were doing, and what they were doing was leading women to Jesus. That's when it hit me: God wanted me to lead the women of our church and somehow, the women of Hawai'i.

I listened more intently to every speaker and to every worship song that was sung, and God was definitely moving inside of me. Priscilla Shirer spoke a message out of Ephesians 3:20-21, "Now all glory to God, who is able, through his mighty power at work within us, to accomplish infinitely more than we might ask or think. Glory to him in the church and in Christ Jesus through all generations forever and ever! Amen." It was so powerfully spoken that this was the message for me at this conference. God was showing me that NOW, today, not tomorrow, but NOW, was the time to rise up. It would be through His mighty power in me that I would accomplish all of the things that He was calling me to do.

At the last session of the conference they played that worship song "Awakening" once again, and it became my anthem song for the year, as well as my prayer. I want to be awakened. I want to rise up! I want to have that extraordinary life that God promised me I would have if I chose to obey Him. As I looked once again at the whole arena, watching 10,000 women worshiping to this song, I thought in my head, "Wouldn't it be awesome if 10,000 women in Hawai'i would worship together like this in one place." And the Lord said, "Go and teach them." I clearly heard His voice, and it almost felt like an assignment was given to me that night. I was to lead the women not only in my church, but the women in my state. Tears started to flow down my checks and my hand was raised up high, as I worshiped with all my heart and soul. A fire was burning inside of me that I could not contain. I heard my next calling, and I was excited for the days ahead.

The conference ended and people were hanging around talking with one another. I just sat there, staring out into space, and couldn't believe all that had just happened to me during this time. I couldn't believe what had happened between our conferences in Hawai'i to this one in Sydney. I saw Lisa Bevere leaving, so I went up to her and tapped her on the shoulder. I didn't say a word, I just looked at her face. She looked at mine and said, "Let's do this!" That's all she had to say to me, and I said, "YES! Let's do this." She hugged me and gave me her phone number and said to call her, and that was the beginning of our friendship. God put her into my world because I believe she would be a mentor to me and to the women of Hawai'i. I believe God will put people in your life who have a similar DNA or share a similar assignment, so we can encourage one another. God allowed me to see and experience this conference because I had never seen a conference like this before; a women's conference that was exciting, vibrant, current, and full of vision and creativity. I thank God that I went to this conference and that I obeyed. I could have just kept adding more and more excuses as to why I couldn't, but instead I gave in to the Holy Spirit and said "yes." How many of us would say we might have missed some opportunities because we allowed the excuses of life and fear to have the best of us? Let's stop making excuses and start allowing God to have His way with our plans and us.

I finally called Mike and told him that I had the best time with God. It was so hard to explain to him just what had happened because I was speechless as to what God had been showing me. I was exhausted because of the time difference and overloaded on God's presence. I was just speechless.

I didn't want the feeling to go away, and had to fight the lies of the enemy that were telling me that it was just an emotional hype. The enemy was saying, "God really didn't speak to you, you were just getting very emotional because of the song." I've gone to church retreats where we would go away for the weekend, and all we did was worship and hear the word of God fed to us non-stop. It was awesome because it's what we need sometimes, a good dose of God vitamins. Usually after coming down from a mountaintop experience, you come to reality and realize you're no longer on that mountain singing worship songs and hearing the word spoken constantly. You're going back to your daily routine and dealing with the same old issues as life continues. This was something I was afraid of happening to me as I headed home from Sydney. I didn't want to share everything with Mike because I wasn't sure if everything that I felt was going to happen. I'm the kind of person who wants to make sure that I mean what I say. I don't want to say something that I am not going to do or live up to. My word is my bond; if I say I'll do something then I'll do it, and if I can't do it then I won't say I can.

Even after the conference in Hawai'i with John Bevere, I wasn't able to articulate what I felt because I was afraid the feelings and emotions would fade away, and I would still be who I was, fearful and intimidated. Isn't that so sad how the enemy can torment us in our thinking? He knows our weaknesses and knows where we are so vulnerable that he will do everything to knock us down and make us feel defeated. The same thing happened right after this conference in Sydney. That's the very reason why I wanted to write this book, because I believe so many of us have heard the call of God in our lives, but the enemy (Satan) comes and steals it from us. Just as the scripture says:

10 *The thief comes only to steal and kill and destroy; I have come that they may have life, and have it to the full.* John 10:10 (NIV)

I remember sitting in my hotel room and just journaling everything I had experienced because I didn't want to forget it. I wanted to remember this moment, and I didn't want it to end. As I talked with Mike over the phone, I literally avoided telling him everything. I just wanted to know how the kids were doing and that I would be home the next day and couldn't wait to tell him everything. I wanted to give myself some time to think about all that had just happened.

I arrived home, and boy had I missed my girls so much! I had never been away this long from them. I was tired and busy with the girls, so Mike and I didn't have much time to talk. I was quiet the next several days because I felt different, and I actually didn't know what to do with what God downloaded in me at the conference. So Mike finally asked me the question, "Honey, tell me about your trip." We sat down in our living room, and I started to share with him what God had been doing in my life. As I shared with him what I had experienced and what God told me, the fire that I had felt at the conference was still inside of me. I started to explain to him that this overwhelming feeling and fire had started when John Bevere came to speak at our conference a month ago. I told him I couldn't shake it, and I couldn't believe that God wanted me to lead the women and to speak to these women. I was tearing up as I shared because I was in awe of what God was doing in my life. I told him I was afraid to tell him because if I did, he would make it happen. I was afraid I would have to act upon what God told me, to lead the women at our church and to start speaking. You see, I never had the desire to lead women's ministries or to speak at all. I always thought women's ministries were boring, and I had spoken at our church a couple of times, but it wasn't my favorite thing to do. I remember at the Hillsong Conference one summer, Mike shared with me that God told him to start having me share in church. I remember looking at him like "you're hilarious and yeah right." In all the years that we had been in ministry, we had never seen a woman preach on the weekend. It wasn't modeled for us to have both the senior pastor and his wife share in church. Our model was only the senior pastor and his male pastoral staff preach in church. I had done communion for the church, but had never shared a message from the bible. This was all new to me until I saw it modeled at Hillsong.

After sharing my adventure with Mike, he said that I would be sharing at our next leadership meeting. I would have said "no" right off the bat, but I already knew that I was supposed to share at that meeting. So I told him "yes" out of obedience to Mike and to God. I didn't do that backstroke routine of trying to get out of it by making all kinds of excuses. There was a part of me that was excited to share my adventure with the leaders because I believed they had all received something out of our conference with John. I would have been surprised if they hadn't, because it was one of the most powerful messages that I've heard. I wanted our leaders to rise up as well, and be obedient to what God revealed to them. So many times we can hear a great message, whether it's in church or a conference, or through your time of journaling, but what do we do with what God tells us? Many of us don't know what to do with what God tells us, so we just sit on it and say, "God did this or that or said this or that," but what do we do with it? I wanted to challenge them, as well as myself, to be obedient and to rise up to our calling TOGETHER. I believe together we can make a bigger impact and be a stronger team.

I finally told Mike all that God had been doing since the time I had been praying months prior to our HNL Conference with John Bevere to attending the Hillsong Colour Women's Conference in Sydney. I spoke it into the atmosphere, and now I was accountable to live out the vision that God gave me. My new journey had begun and I was freaking out because I didn't know what I was doing, and that's not normal. I usually have to know everything before I act upon anything because I don't like surprises, and I don't like not knowing the plans. I like to have everything in my control, but this time, God was in control and I had to lean on Him and trust Him once again. I promised God that I didn't want to lead a women's ministry that was boring, but a ministry of women that will rise up and live out their full potential in Christ while making an impact both locally and globally. Now the hard work would begin; assembling of a team of women who would help me lead the women of our church.

CHAPTER NINE

ARISE, NOW IS THE TIME!

As God's fellow workers, we urge you not to receive God's grace in vain. For he says, "In the time of my favor I heard you, and in the day of salvation I helped you." I tell you, NOW IS THE TIME of God's favor, NOW is the day of salvation. **2 Corinthians 6:1 (NIV)**

"Arise! For this matter is your responsibility but we will be with you. Be courageous and act." **Ezra 10:4**

Mike had asked me to share everything with the leaders of our church at our monthly leadership night. As I was preparing for this night, I was so nervous because this was so new to me. I was glad that Mike helped me prepare a message with scriptures and illustrations to help communicate what God had downloaded to me.

That night, no one really knew that I was going to speak. Worship began and I pleaded with God to somehow let me out of this. My stomach was turning into knots, and my brain was overloaded with the fear that I would forget what I had written in my notes. I remember driving over to the church and listening to John Bevere's teaching on "Breaking Intimidation" because I needed to overcome it, right then and there. I needed John to yell at me with the scriptures and tell me that I am graced to do this. I needed constant reminders about who I was in Christ, and that the power of the Holy Spirit was in me to do all things in Jesus' name. Apparently, I was not alone because Mike said that anyone who has to preach goes through this all the time. I knew this was a process I had to go through, and I wanted to be obedient to God. I wanted to change how I responded to fear; instead of running away from fear, I wanted to overcome it and prevent it from taking hold of me and keeping me from doing what God had called me to do.

I believe that so many of us deal with this issue of fear. Fear actually holds us back from doing anything. I like what Paul says to Timothy in 2 Timothy 1:7 (NLT) "For God has not given us a spirit of fear and timidity, but of power, love, and self-discipline." Knowing God's truth will set us free, and if only we would continue to believe in this truth, we could do so much more for Jesus.

Worship ended, and Mike introduced me by sharing a little about what God had been doing in my life. I went up and my voice was cracking so badly because I was scared as I spoke. I started sharing all that had happened to me since our HNL conference with John Bevere and my trip to Sydney. It was a raw message in which I shared everything about how I felt. From feeling insecure to God speaking to me about leading the women in our church, and how much I wanted to be obedient to what God was asking of me. I challenged all of our leaders that night to come forward if they felt the same way about wanting to be obedient when God asks them to do something. I believed that God had been speaking to all of us, but so many times we allow the devil to take away what

God has said to us by telling us lies. The devil likes to plant seeds of doubt in our minds to confuse us about what we've heard from God. As I called them up, many of the leaders came forward, and 75% of them came forward to receive prayer. Many of them had tears in their eyes because they knew they had been disobedient by not doing what God has called them to do. Many have had visions from God to do something for years, but had not done anything about them because of the seeds of doubt and fear of the unknown.

After the service, I had men and women come up to me to say "thank you," for sharing what God put on my heart for our church. A woman came up to me and said that God had been asking her to start a ministry for young girls to teach them about purity, so I connected her to our youth pastor and she taught the girls about purity. Another woman came up to me and said that she loved sewing and knew that God wanted her to help people through sewing. She ended up starting a ministry, with many other ladies in the church, sewing clothes, blankets, and other items to help the needy. Another lady approached me and said that she liked to bake and ended up starting up a ministry called "Bake a Blessing," in which she bakes birthday cakes for boys who are in a detention facility because many of the their parents had forgotten about their birthdays. I had other women and men start up ministries in response to what God had told them about years ago, and now many other people are being helped through these very same ministries.

A woman named Julie, started a ministry for kids called, "Kids Rock" in a poor area near our church. These kids play in the park with no parental supervision every day because many of their parents are not present, or they're being taken care of by a grandparent who already has many other children to care for. She had a vision from God to start a Sunday school in the park on

Saturdays. This ministry has grown and a team of volunteers is now serving faithfully each weekend to minister to these children and their families. I could go on and on and tell you about other people rising up to their callings. This is one of my passions, to see people do what God has called them to do.

We have a saying that we borrowed from Pastor Miles McPherson of The Rock Church in San Diego: "DO SOMETHING." We believe each one of us is an answer to the problems of this world, and we ALL can do something with what God has given us. We have talents and gifts and we must use them to serve others. 1 Corinthians 12:7 (NLT) "A spiritual gift is given to each of us so we can help each other." Each one of us is uniquely made in God's image and has been given many gifts and talents. There is so much to do on this earth and not enough people to get it done. 1 Timothy 4:14-16 says, "Do not neglect the spiritual gift you received through the prophecy spoken over you when the elders of the church laid their hands on you. Give your complete attention to these matters. Throw yourself into your tasks so that everyone will see your progress. Keep a close watch on how you live and on your teaching. Stay true to what is right for the sake of your own salvation and the salvation of those who hear you."

After that night someone came up to me and said, "You're different, and there is a glow about you." I told him, "Yes, I am different and it's so hard to explain, but I'm so on fire for the Lord." When you decide to obey the Lord and step out in faith, your life will change. His presence will go before you, and you just have to follow. As you step out, others will do the same. It's unbelievable what God wants to do through His people. He wants willing vessels to be His hands and feet. God puts the passion and fire inside of us to fulfill the destiny that He has designed for each one of us.

Now I had to begin the work of assembling a team of women who would help me fulfill the vision that God gave me. I had lunch with one of the girls on my team named Liane, and shared with her the vision that I saw for our women. I shared that I wanted to have a monthly women's night with worship and teaching and a yearly conference with guest speakers from around the world. I had a name for the ministry, but wasn't satisfied with it because it didn't sound right. I told her I wanted something like "RISE UP" women's ministry. I know, that doesn't sound great! I just couldn't find the right wording, but that was my thought behind the name. I wanted women to rise up, but I didn't know what they should rise up to? As I shared this with her, she looked overwhelmed and speechless. I knew something started to stir inside of her because I could see it. It was a big vision, and I knew I couldn't do it without a team. She would be one of my major players because she would be able to help me organize these services and this conference.

About a month later, Mike was at a conference in New Zealand and had met some great pastors from all over the world. He called me and mentioned that he met a couple named Shane and Georgie Baxter of Enjoy Church in Melbourne, Australia, in the van as they were being driven to the conference. He couldn't stop talking about how great this guy was and how well they got along. He told me to look them up on their church website to see who they were, so I did. I scrolled through their website and found their women's ministry page, and noticed the name of their ministry, ADORE. For some reason, something hit me when I saw that name. I noticed it was one word and it was a powerful word, so I came to the conclusion that the name that I would pick for our women's ministry would be one word as well. So, I looked up the phrase 'rise up" and found different synonym words for it, but the word that caught my eye was, ARISE. When I saw that word, I knew that was the name of our ministry. I loved it! So ARISE it was, and I shared it with my team and they loved it as well. So thanks, Shane and Georgie!!!

We got confirmation that Lisa Bevere and her husband, John, would be the first speakers at our very first Arise conference in January of the cominglike year. To prepare the ladies for the conference, I felt that we needed to have two services beforehand so that I could teach them what it means to rise up to all that God has for us. Our first gathering was in September, and the team and I had prepared a great night of worship, connecting, and a message that I would share. This would be my first time sharing with the women, and I was so nervous and scared. I know how women can be; they can be critical and judgmental of one another and that's what I was afraid of. I have to be honest; I was dealing with so many insecurities and lies that were going through my head about my ability to communicate and their acceptance of me, that it was causing me much anxiety and lack of sleep. I prayed and prayed, and that was all I could do.

There was a buzz about this Arise service all around our church, as well as at other churches. Ladies were wondering what this event was going to be all about. I felt the pressure of making sure this night was going to be awesome, and that it wouldn't be the last, but the first of many nights for the ladies. I wanted God to be present and for Him to do something inside each of us. I couldn't wait to see the result of our first Arise service.

We thought maybe 200 ladies would show up to our first service, but as the worship began that night, women were coming in non-stop, and the ushers had to set up more chairs. We underestimated ourselves. We were so surprised by how many ladies attended – there were over 400 ladies that night at our first service. The buzz of excitement was definitely in the air that night. Women came expectant and were curious as to what this Arise conference was all about.

As I was worshiped, I asked God to have my back and asked Him to help me speak well and help me not be so nervous. I was literally freaking out because my husband was freaking out. I noticed him getting out of his seat to make sure the service was running well, and then I saw him telling my team what to do. I think he was just as nervous as I was, and he wasn't speaking. He wanted to make sure everything was running the way it should be, and he was just as shocked at how many ladies showed up. As worship was ending, Mike went up to introduce me, and I began to cry a little because I was so touched by his words. The ladies stood up and honored me and that made me cry even more. What a way to start a message – me crying.

The ladies were responsive and listened intently to what I had to say. I spoke about the Arise ministry and what I had seen for us women. I saw a generation of women being released by God and rising up to their full expression in Him and making an impact in this world. God is calling us to arise!

The definition of arise is to come into being; rise to one's feet; move forward; get up, and rise. To arise is to awake. Ephesians 5:14 (NIV) says, "Wake up, O sleeper, rise from the dead, and Christ will shine on you." I believe I had been asleep for a while to the things of God. I was busy raising my kids and leading a church with my husband and just living the normal life, but I was still asleep to things of God. I believe God has been trying to get our attention for a long time, but His children are not listening. Romans 13:11-14 (MSG) says, "But make sure that you don't get so absorbed and exhausted in taking care of all your day-by-day obligations that you lose track of the time and doze off, oblivious to God. The night is about over, dawn is about to break. Be up and awake to what God is doing! God is putting the finishing touches on the salvation work he began when we first believed. We can't afford to waste a minute, must not squander these precious daylight hours in frivolity and indulgence, in sleeping around and dissipation, in bickering and grabbing everything in sight. Get out of bed and get dressed! Don't loiter and linger, waiting until the very last minute. Dress yourselves in Christ, and be up and about!"

I can give you an example of what it means to be asleep. My husband once slept through a tsunami siren. This was during our HNL conference with John Bevere and Ben Houston. It was our final day of conference, and we were notified of a possible tsunami headed our way. We were all tired from the night before because we came home late from the conference. I'm not a heavy sleeper, but Mike can be. As I slept, I heard sirens going off, but I didn't know what they were for. Then about 6 a.m. my phone rang, but I failed to pick it up in time. Our executive pastor, Mark Peterman, left a message that a tsunami was expected to hit us around 10 a.m., and he wanted to know what we should do about the conference. I started to panic because our guest speakers were staying at a hotel right on the beach. If a tsunami did hit us, they would get hit first. So, I walked back to our bedroom and saw Mike sleeping and snoring away. I told him, more like shouted, "Wake up!!" He was startled by the way I woke him up. Honestly, I couldn't believe he could sleep through those sirens and the phone ringing so early in the morning. Just imagine if there was a robber trying to break into our house, I don't think he would be able to hear that robber. I told him, "Didn't you hear those sirens? There's a tsunami coming this morning, and John and Ben are at the hotel." He woke up and was a little puzzled at what I said, so I had to repeat myself. He finally listened to the message on the phone and called John and Ben. Their rooms were on the higher floors, so they would be okay. He made a decision to cancel the conference because we were told not to be driving on the roads. Mike felt that he needed to be at the church because our church would be a place for people who needed shelter. Mike headed to church and later called me to say that some people had actually shown up for the conference. I couldn't believe that. I guess if you've had several tsunami warnings without anything serious happen (like we have), you tend to not take the warning seriously.

God has been setting off the sirens in our life, but we can't hear them or we choose not to hear them. We've been sleeping through the sirens, but it's time to wake up.

Back to our first Arise service, God was surely with me as I spoke and shared my heart for the women. I challenged them to rise up to everything that God had for them and to be set free from the things that held them captive. Things such as fear, intimidation, self-worth, past sins, anger, and many others that hold us back from living a life of freedom. I shared with them my struggles with intimidation and fear, and how they had kept me imprisoned in my thoughts. I gave them a picture of what it looks like to be imprisoned when we actually are not. The picture was of a dog on a leash. When she was a puppy, I wanted to take her outside, so I leashed her, as any owner would do. My neighbor was outside, and we were sitting in the carport with my dog on the leash, and she told me to unleash her. I told her that if I did, she would run away. She then said, "The dog won't know you've unleashed her, she'll still think that it's on because it's been on her for a while." This is a picture of someone who thinks she's leashed to (imprisoned by) her past sins, unworthiness, fears, and intimidation, when in fact she's actually been set free because of what Jesus did on the cross for us. Many of us walk around like we have a leash on that holds us back from living the life that God has for us. The truth is that we are no longer bound to our sins and fears, but we are free in Christ. Galatians 5:1 (MSG) says that, "Christ has set us free to live a free life. So take your stand! Never again let anyone put a harness of slavery on you."

God's presence was definitely in the room at the end of our first Arise service. Ladies were in awe, and many were set free that night. There was a new sense of freedom as we ended the service with worship. There was a difference from when the ladies came at the beginning of the service to worship; they were shy, timid, and had their walls up. After the message and altar call, the ladies were jumping and raising their hands up high and many danced as they worshiped. I sensed freedom for the ladies and for myself. I told the ladies that we would do this together. We will arise together, and we will let nothing hold us back from becoming all that God calls us to be.

Although the first Arise service had just ended and the ladies were being set free, the process of staying free had begun. To keep arising we needed God to work in us and change us. I never want to be complacent in my relationship with God, and I want to keep growing and becoming more like Christ, but the process is going to be real. I still had more truths to unveil about myself because the fears and intimidation were hard to overcome. But I wasn't going to give up. I wanted to ARISE to my full expression in Christ.

CHAPTER TEN

IS THAT A TRUTH OR A LIE?

4 *"Do not be afraid; you will not be put to shame. Do not fear disgrace; you will not be humiliated.*

Isaiah 54:4 (NIV)

God rescued me in 1990, and I am so thankful that He is in my life. I am forever changed, and I have purpose and a destiny on my life. I would never have guessed my life would be where it is today. I am married to one of the greatest leaders in the state of Hawai'i and a fabulous father to my daughters. My life is rich in every way, and I thank God for enlarging my world with Arise.

I love leading women because we are all alike in so many ways. We struggle with the same issues in life, and we have so many insecurities and fears that often hold us back from becoming everything God intends for us to be. I realize the truth about how we women can be so fake at times with one another. We pretend we have it all together, when we actually don't. We compare ourselves to one another because we have been doing it since we were preteens. We never think we are good enough, or something is always not right in our lives. It could be how we look, how much we weigh, how smart or how popular we are, or who we date. Sometimes I think we never outgrow our childish behavior of comparison. I've always wanted to be like someone else because I wasn't happy with who I was. As I shared in previous chapters, I didn't want to be different from all the normal people; I wanted to be accepted by them. Society and media have modeled an accepted image of women of what we should look like, dress like, and act like. I've watched too many shows and movies and read too many romance books that literally tainted my view of what a woman should be.

As a child, I did not have mentors in my life that spoke truth to me; instead, I believed in lies about who I was, and not who I was meant to be. I wasn't a Christian growing up; therefore, I didn't have the privilege of knowing God's truth about who I was and could be in Christ. I'm so thankful that my daughters have grown up with the knowledge of the word of God because they have been given the truth about who they truly are. All youth programs are so vital for our children because they provide role models they can look up to and people to speak truth into them and about who they are in Christ. One of my passions in life is speaking truth to those who have believed a lie about themselves and who they are. I learned how to recognize the lies that I've believed about myself through a study I did years ago by Beth Moore. Through the study, I identified the lies and didn't want to be controlled by these lies anymore; I wanted to be free. In her book entitled, *Breaking Free*, there's a chapter that spoke so loudly to me that it literally changed my life. It taught what it meant to be held captive to the lies of the enemy and how to be set free. The first step is recognizing the captor or the lie; second, standing in agreement with God; third, tearing down the lies or strongholds; fourth, building up the truth; and finally, surrendering the thoughts to the truth. It was a vivid picture of what it would look like if you and I were standing in a small room, almost like a prison cell, which represented the lies that you and I have believed about ourselves such as, "I am not pretty, smart, worthy, accepted, forgiven, or good enough, etc." The lies formed the walls. And each wall was being built, brick by brick, lie upon lie, until we are hemmed in on every side. The enemy wants you to think you are stuck in that room forever with no way out. The truth is, there is a way out of that room! You don't have to be held captive in that room because there has always been a door already opened to you! All we need to do is open that door because we've had the key (God's Word) to unlock it the whole time. The key is Jesus and His truth will set us free. This picture was so clear to me, and I realized how lies had held me captive for so long. I wanted to be free, so I used the key to unlock myself to freedom. I didn't want these lies to continue living rent free in my thoughts and my life. I wanted to evict them for good! I will never allow the adversary access to my life again.

Let me share with you some of the lies I have believed, and hopefully this will help you to recognize some of the lies in your life, as well as know the truth that will set you free. I am being vulnerable with you because I want to be, because I know you and I are no different. You and I want to be set free, and when God sets us free, we are able to help others be set free. The biggest lie I had to recognize was not being smart enough. I know what you're thinking, "WHAT? REALLY?" It was important to me to be smart because it showed how good I was in academics. I didn't like it when the teacher would hand back our tests because I would see a lot of red marks on mine, and oftentimes, grades that were lower than a C. I would look over to see what my friends got, and they always had better grades than me. I would often hide my test papers so no one would see what I had received. I was embarrassed, and I hated being graded on everything I did. I wanted to be like the smart girls who had A's and B's. After graduating from a two-year college, I worked full-time at a hotel in Waikiki. I met so many people while working at the hotel, and many thought I had graduated with a bachelor's degree because I looked smart. I was always ashamed to tell people I didn't have a bachelor's degree because I believed it would make me look unintelligent. As you know, I come from a Chinese family who had high expectations for us to do well in school and marry someone who made lots of money and had a title, like a doctor or something comparable. My parents were blunt and not very encouraging, rather more critical and judgmental. Please don't get me wrong, they are great people who did really well in life without speaking any English and coming to Hawai'i and building a successful television repair shop. They weren't mean people, just people who spoke the truth with no tact. In America, you would call that being rude, but in a Chinese family it wasn't considered rude, it was normal. As a child, it didn't bother me that my parents didn't encourage me or speak highly of me because that was the way it was. I never knew any better. My parents never told me I was smart, only that I was pretty. My older sister, on the other hand, was told she was smart. So I assumed I wasn't smart, which is what I believed for a long time about myself. I didn't do as well in school as my older sister did. I was your typical average kid who passed with C's and some B's, but I wanted to be considered smart. I guess I looked smart because I was Chinese. In my school the Chinese students, as well as other Asian students, were considered the smart ones in school. I don't want to pigeonhole people based on their ethnicity, but that was the way we saw Asians in my school.

The truth to combat the lie that I wasn't smart is that I am smart, wise, knowledgeable, and capable to do all things in Christ. Philippians 4:13 (NLT) declares, "For I can do EVERYTHING through Christ who gives me strength." This truth has allowed me to want to learn and grow in my knowledge of the bible, and so many other things that I want to know about. Do I like school? Still, no, I don't. I like to learn, I just don't want to be graded on it, like a test. Learning is fun now because I have my own expectation to be smarter and because I want to know things, and not because I have to.

One day as my connect group was doing the "*Breaking Free*" study, we each began sharing with one another a lie that we had believed about ourselves. It was very humbling for all of us to be vulnerable with each other. I had to start first because if I didn't, I'm not sure if anyone would have been truthful. I was so nervous about sharing what I had walked through because this would be the first time that I would be sharing with a group of ladies about my inadequacies, and I really felt embarrassed to say that I had believed I was not smart enough. As I shared this lie, the ladies were so accepting rather than judgmental of me. I thought they would laugh or be shocked that I didn't graduate from a four-year college. It was so freeing for me because I was so ashamed to have believed such a lie for so long, but that's how the enemy works. He wants to make you think that everyone will laugh and judge you if you tell anyone, anything of significance. The enemy wants to keep you in that prison; make you think you there's no way out, but there is a way out. Confessing to a group of ladies you trust is so freeing. Once you confess the lies, thoughts, or struggles, they're immediately exposed to the light, and the truth can come in and erase, as well as replace that lie. I no longer have to pretend that I graduated from a four-year college, but can be open about it and not feel ashamed about simply graduating from a two-year college. I learned that God will never shame you or embarrass you, and that's the truth as it is said in Isaiah 54:4: "Do not be afraid; you will not be put to shame. Do not fear disgrace; you will not be humiliated." As the other ladies shared their lie, I could see freedom in the room. It was like a veil was lifted off their faces and truth came in as the lie went out. That was the beginning of my freedom in Christ.

Another lie the enemy had convinced me of was that I had to be perfect in man's image. I couldn't show my weaknesses or insecurities. I had to pretend that I had it all together. I wanted to please people and I wanted them to accept me. I didn't like being corrected because it showed my inadequacies. I realized later that it was pride keeping me from growing and learning. The root of the lie that I had to be perfect in man's image was wanting to be accepted by others. This can be traced back to my childhood when I was in a class for kids who were different. This lie carried me throughout my school days and into adulthood, and I believe many are carrying this lie inside of us. We perform for others so we can get approval, and that approval tells us that we are accepted. I never thought people's comments or approval were that important to me until I realized the root cause was that I felt I had to be perfect. Now, as a Christian, I've learned to please God rather than man. If I was to please man all the time, I would be disappointed and exhausted, but if I choose to please God, He will always accept me as I am. He will love me in spite of my inadequacies, fears, mistakes, and imperfections. I learned it was okay to not be okay with myself and with others.

God also exposed another lie to me during this season of rising up. The lie was that white (Caucasian) men are more powerful than Asian people. My dad told me as a child that white men were powerful because they had money and titles and we didn't. Interestingly, I've had white men as bosses, and they were very intimidating to me. I always felt I was not smart enough to hold a conversation with them, and I would shy away from them whenever I was around them. I kept my conversations with them as short as possible because I didn't want them to know that I couldn't understand what they were talking about. I didn't feel I had enough smarts to carry a conversation with them. I'm fairly sure that's why I dated guys who were not Caucasian, but rather Asian or mixed-raced. It's so funny because when I became a Christian, my pastor was a Caucasian man. He intimidated me every time he stood by the exit door as we left church. I didn't want to have a conversation with him, but he would always make it a point to talk to me after services. I always kept it short, but he was different from the men I've talked with. He was kind and gentle and didn't make me feel inadequate or lesser than. He was very interested in my life and how I was doing. Pastor Ralph really helped me break the lie that not all Caucasian men are intimidating. He helped me grow as a young Christian and believed in me by allowing me to serve in a leadership capacity in the church. He saw leadership gifting inside of me and was my biggest cheerleader as I led the children's ministry for 12 years at Hope Chapel Kaneohe Bay. Once this area was revealed and the lie broken, I was able to speak to Caucasian men and not feel intimidated. And guess what? I married a man who was part Caucasian with additional ethnicities such as Italian, Filipino, Hawai'ian, Chinese, Norwegian, and Scottish. We call these people 'hapa,' which is a Hawai'ian word for mixed-race. I married a hapa guy, and a good-looking hapa guy. He doesn't intimidate me at all. Interestingly enough, now that I often speak at church, there are men and women in the audience that I used to be so intimidated by, but not so much now. Caucasian men have come up to me several times and have said the messages I've spoken at church have hit home for them or that they got something out of them. Their approval of me was very important to me and that's how God was showing me that I no longer have to be intimidated by them. I am accepted because God has already accepted me. Isn't God so good? He knows all of our insecurities and fears, and He knows how to speak to us and help us through the journey to freedom.

I want to share one last lie that I believe most of us have probably believed about ourselves at some point or another. I always felt like I was not important enough. I felt like my comments didn't matter, my presence wasn't noticed, or I was forgotten. My mom said that as a little girl, I was very quiet, to the point that no one knew I was in the room. I didn't make a big fuss as a little girl, so I was assumed to be a good girl. I always minded my own business and watched everyone else talk while I listened. I would consider myself an observer and not so much a talker. Growing up and having many different groups of friends, allowed me to hide in some ways. I was never the leader of the group, just a person who tagged along and went with the flow. Every once in a while, if I really didn't like something, I would say so. I guess you could say that I am an easy-going type of person. So whenever I am with a crowd of people, I tend not to say much. That's my personality, but somehow this made me feel like no one noticed me, and I can see why – because I was never really the outspoken one in the group. I somehow believed in a lie that I was not important enough and therefore, was not noticed by the people in my groups. I could easily hide behind that lie, but that wasn't true about who I was. I had things to say, but I didn't say them because I thought no one was interested in what I had to say. I hope this makes sense to you. Oftentimes, I asked myself this question, "Does anyone know I exist?" I remember attending a Hillsong Conference, I believe it was my second or third conference, and I didn't know many people sitting in my area. I felt a little uncomfortable because I had no one to really talk to. As I sat there, I thought about how no one knows me, but then all of a sudden, God spoke to me and whispered, "I KNOW YOU, AND YOU KNOW ME." I felt so special right then and there. Of all the people that were at the conference, God picked me out and said that to me. The conference was beginning and Pastor Brian Houston, who is the senior pastor of Hillsong Church (and who was just at our church a week prior to this conference), started to speak. He looked at my section where I was sitting and recognized me in front of 10,000 women. I wanted to shrink back into my seat, but I didn't. I was like, "WOW, he knows me, and he called my name." I was sitting close to Lisa Bevere, who was in the section next to me and a couple of rows up, and she looked at me and gave me a nod like, "Wow, that's good." Sometimes we just need to be reminded that it doesn't matter if anyone knows you because God already knows you. He knows all about you, and he loves you just as you are. You matter to HIM! He notices you when no one else does. He finds you when no one else is looking. He sees what you are doing, and He is so proud of you. That's our Father!!

Psalm 139:14 (NKJV) *says,* "I will praise You, for I am fearfully *and* wonderfully made; Marvelous are Your works, and *that* my soul knows very well."

Why am I sharing with you the lies that I had believed about myself? It's because I believe that you also may have believed in some of these lies or others that I've not mentioned. Confessing them to someone or to your connect group is a great start in your walk to freedom. When you confess with your mouth and hear what you're saying, you'll come to understand that this lie that you have believed for so long is so untrue! The devil wants to keep you captive to those lies for as long as he can so you won't fulfill the calling and destiny that God has for your life. The devil will do whatever he can to hold you back and occupy your time, energy, and thoughts on the things that are not true. Instead, let God occupy your mind with truth!

"Summing it all up, friends, I'd say you'll do best by filling your minds and meditating on things true, noble, reputable, authentic, compelling, gracious—the best, not the worst; the beautiful, not the ugly; things to praise, not things to curse. Put into practice what you learned from me, what you heard and saw and realized. Do that, and God, who makes everything work together, will work you into his most excellent harmonies." Philippians 4:8-9 (MSG)

I have a saying with my kids, "Is that a truth or a lie?" Anytime my daughters come to me and say things like, "I'm stupid, I'm not pretty, I'm not smart, I'm this or that," I ask them that question. I need them to really understand what they are saying, and they need to determine if it is really a truth or a lie. I don't want them to go on in life believing in the same lies I did when I was their age. I have the truth in the word of God, and I will use that truth to set my girls free. This was something I didn't have in my life growing up. No one told me the truth, but no one also knew the lies that I had believed because I didn't have the right people in my life to share them with. I have many friends that can do that for me now, and my kids have so many great aunties and uncles in their life that all speak truth to them. The lies of the enemy can shake up a person and rattle them into insecurity, pride, and shame. I want to help people break those lies and speak truth over their lives, so they may live in peace with who they are in Christ. I've become very bold about this, and if someone I am counseling believes in a lie about themselves, I will ask them the same question that I ask my daughters, "IS THIS A TRUTH OR A LIE?"

9 *Truthful words stand the test of time, but lies are soon exposed.* **Proverbs 12:19(NLT)**

Let me ask you the same question about the lies you have believed about yourself, "IS THAT A TRUTH OR A LIE?" When you answer the question, ask yourself if what you have believed is the actual truth, because you have to believe the truth about what God says about you in order to be set free. God's truth will stand the test of time, but lies will soon be exposed, as Proverbs 12:19 says. Let's not continue on in life believing in a lie, but walk in the truth about who God says we are.

11 *For I know the plans I have for you," says the Lord. "They are plans for good and not for disaster, to give you a future and a hope.* **Jeremiah 29:11 (NLT)**

After I spoke at our first Arise event, I knew that there was more speaking to come with the second Arise event, and then the conference with John and Lisa Bevere. Each time I spoke, fear and intimidation would come over me; fear of people judging me and saying the wrong thing. I actually hated the fact that I went through this each time that I spoke. I continue to battle the same lies in my mind, and it caused me so much anxiety. I didn't want to be caught in a web of lies anymore, but wanted to exchange all of the lies for God's truth. I knew there would be more that would surface, but I now knew how to deal with them. I often had to remind myself that grace was all I needed to do this, and that Jesus had my back and He wouldn't shame me. I had to continue to be obedient to the calling upon my life to lead women and to help women overcome their battles with insecurities and fears. I wanted freedom from bondage to the lies that I had believed for so long. It was a process that I had to go through because without going through the process, I would not have been able to walk fully in the truth of who I am in Christ. The journey of walking this calling out was often painful, but each time I spoke to the ladies, the reward of seeing the ladies set free was always worth it. I was willing to overcome my insecurities and fears as long as it would help others be set free. I was willing to be transparent with the women because that allowed them to do the same.

I had to learn to walk in my authority and know who lives inside of me every day until I could manage my insecurities and intimidation and overcome them with the truth of the word. I wrote scriptures on 3x5 note cards, and I read books by John and Lisa Bevere, Paul and Maree de Jong, Bobbie Houston, Priscilla Shirer, David McCracken, and so many others to remind myself of who I was and who I am in Christ. I attended conferences and wrote all of the thoughts God had of me, so I wouldn't forget. I wanted to keep growing, and I wanted to overcome my fears, so I could rise up to my fullness in Christ. It was time that I grew up and took my position as a leader and shepherd. My work is not done, there's more to do and more women to be set free.

CHAPTER ELEVEN

TAG, YOU'RE IT

58 *With all this going for us, my dear, dear friends, stand your ground. And don't hold back. Throw yourselves into the work of the Master, confident that nothing you do for him is a waste of time or effort.*

1 Corinthians 15:58 (MSG)

As young girls, we often played a game called "tag," where you run and someone chases after you, and once they tag you, it's your turn to tag someone else. The goal is not to get tagged. Oftentimes, we are running away from getting tagged by God to lead or to serve the body of Christ. We always think someone else will do it, or we'll just wait until someone else answers the call. So many of us are running away from the calling upon our lives. A man named Jonah, in the bible was running away from God, so he was swallowed up by a whale in order for God to get his attention. His calling was to tell the people of Nineveh about their disobedience and that God wanted them saved. Another man named Moses, ran away from God, but God called him back because he was the man called to lead God's people out of slavery and into the promised land that God had for them. How many of us can relate to these stories? I love Moses' excuse of "I can't speak Lord, I don't know what to say." He questioned his ability to lead the people and to speak. So many people in the bible ran away from their callings until God captured their hearts. You and I are captured by His heart because He rescued us and gave us lives that have purpose, hope, peace, and love. He also gave us talents and gifts to be used for the kingdom. He created us, and He knows what we can do.

When Pastor Ralph asked me to lead the children's ministry when I was just a new believer, I thought that there was no way I could do it. I had every right to decline based on my experience and maturity as a Christian, but because of how I had led an event for the singles ministry, it proved to my pastor that I was in fact, a leader. I was able to gather a team and execute the vision, and the event was successful. He also noticed how I was able to invite people to come along and serve alongside me. This was something I did naturally, which I didn't know was called "leadership." That's why I was offered the position to lead the children's ministry, because it takes a person with that kind of leadership to run a ministry with many servants. I was good at finding and equipping people for the ministry. Many of us don't know what we are gifted with, and it usually takes serving others to determine how we are gifted. If I hadn't been serving in the church, no one would have noticed my spiritual gifting.

It is no coincidence that I am now leading Arise women's ministry at Inspire Church. My role is to gather and equip the ladies for ministry. I'm in a different season in my life now because I'm older and a more mature Christian than when I led the children's ministry. I thank God for these opportunities to serve in the church because I have learned so much about serving people. I love helping others find their giftings and their callings in life and ministry. I believe we all have assignments here on the earth, and we need to complete those assignments. These assignments are our callings in life. We all belong to the same body, with different gifts and talents that make up the body of Christ. No gift is greater than another; every gift is important and useful. God will call some to be apostles, prophets, teachers, some to do miracles, some to have the gift of healing, some who can help others, some to have the gift of leadership, and some to speak in unknown languages, as it says in 1 Corinthians 12:27-31 (NLT):

27 All of you together are Christ's body, and each of you is a part of it. **28** Here are some of the parts God has appointed for the church: first are apostles, second are prophets, third are teachers, then those who do miracles, those who have the gift of healing, those who can help others, those who have the gift of leadership, those who speak in unknown languages. **29** Are we all apostles? Are we all prophets? Are we all teachers? Do we all have the power to do miracles? **30** Do we all have the gift of healing? Do we all have the ability to speak in unknown languages? Do we all have the ability to interpret unknown languages? Of course not! **31** So you should earnestly desire the most helpful gifts.

We need them all, and we need everyone to do their part. Imagine if we all did our part and used the gifting that God gave us? The church would be thriving and growing and many would be saved. My heart's desire is to see this happen through our church and through the Arise ministry that God has positioned me to lead. Arise has grown in the last seven years, and I believe it's a movement of women rising up to their full expression in Christ and making an impact locally here in Hawai'i, and globally.

We started with one Arise conference a year, and now we hold two back-to-back conferences every February. I believe the Lord is enlarging our capacity for more women to become equipped to do everything God is calling them to do. When something gets enlarged, it gets stretched. When God wants to enlarge us, God wants to stretch us. No one loves stretch marks, and I have lots by my stomach area because I birthed two girls. Every stretch mark represents the different growth stages of what was birthed. God was growing Arise, and He was enlarging our capacity for the more that was coming.

> *"Enlarge the place of your tent, And let them* **stretch** *out the curtains of your dwellings; Do not spare; Lengthen your cords, And strengthen your stakes.*   **Is 54:2**

God was preparing us little by little, until we could handle the growth and have two conferences back-to-back. God is preparing you and I little by little, so He can give us more. You might be thinking, "I don't want more, I have enough stretch marks." I'm not talking about having more babies; God wants to enlarge your life. Sometimes, I think the older we get, the less stretchable we are. We don't like change or growth because it causes us to get uncomfortable. No one likes to be uncomfortable, but why stay complacent? There's so much more to learn about ourselves, and so much more that God wants to do through us for His kingdom. We can't stop growing now. It doesn't matter what age you are, we need to continually be growing and stretching beyond our limits.

Sometimes we limit ourselves when it comes to what God can do in us. I have realized that there is a process to change. When change happens it will get uncomfortable, and everything has to shift to adapt to those changes. When I decided to step into the calling of leading the Arise ministry, it was a stretch for me because I knew life would get a lot busier, and I wasn't sure if I could put one more thing on my plate that was already full with leading a church with Mike, and everything that comes with being a wife and a mom. Life was comfortable, my routines were all set, and things were good – so why would I have wanted more in life?

As I said in the beginning, I was seeking the Lord for my next season because I knew God had something more for me do. I didn't know that God was going to ask me to lead the women of our church, but I wanted to do whatever He told me to do. Did I know what was ahead of me? No. I just did what God asked me to do. Was it hard for me? Yes. The hardest thing for me was change because God wanted to change *me.* God wanted to do something inside of me that would grow me and stretch me to become who I am today. It was uncomfortable being the leader of women because I had to share my life with them and allow them to see the flaws in my life. I still remember sharing with the ladies at our first Arise event about how uncomfortable I was sharing a message onstage. I wanted to be confident in front of them, but instead I was so nervous that I kept saying the phrase, "you know what I mean" after every sentence. I wasn't sure if people understood what I had said. After I spoke that night, ladies came up to me and thanked me for being real and authentic with them. I was relieved that they accepted me in spite of my flaws.

I believe so many of us want authenticity in our relationships, yet so many of us are not willing to be real with one another. One of the biggest challenges I experienced myself, was allowing myself to be changed in front of these women. It was humbling and yet so freeing to be vulnerable, open, and honest with these ladies, whom I call my sisters. I know that every lady in that room struggles with the same things in life. They struggle with their worth, identity, beauty, intelligence, and being accepted by others. When we allow ourselves to open up our lives to one another, we will feel safe to be who we actually are. I had a lot of changing to do in my life, and these changes were good changes.

I had to change the way that I looked at myself and the way that I wanted to lead the women. I wanted to be confident, not in myself, but in God; I wanted to have a **Godfidence** (God confidence). We can be confident by ourselves and say that it's all about us, but having a Godfidence is relying totally on God to give you that confidence. To have this Godfidence, you must allow God to have His way with you and help you change your perspective about yourself, and help you overcome your insecurities. Many of our insecurities exist because we don't understand who we are, so we compare ourselves to one another because we want to be like someone else.

If you are willing to let God to stretch you, change is part of the process. I promise you, the changes are good for you. Change is like peeling the layers of your old skin off and having God renew your skin with fresh new layers that are plump and wrinkle-free. As I was going through the process of change, and God was stretching me to my limits, I found a new normal. The life that I thought was normal then, is now different because of all of the changes that have happened with Arise and how God has changed me. This new life has become my new normal. Every change in your life creates a new normal, helping you to avoid complacency in life until the next stretch that God has for you. So, stretch marks are good because they represent change and growth. Let's welcome those stretch marks and be proud of them!

As I said earlier, we all have gifts and talents that need to be used for the kingdom. I love seeing women serve the body of Christ in the church and outside of the church. I believe we all can't serve just inside of the church, but we must serve those outside of the church. I encourage ladies to get involved in organizations that they feel compelled to be a part of and make a difference there. Serve the people that God has called you to serve. There is so much to do in this world, but not enough servants to do it. That's why I titled this chapter, "TAG, YOU'RE IT!" because you are the one that God has called as the answer to the problems of this world. You are made for so much more than what you think you are. You matter to God and to this generation. Every generation has its time to bear God's light. This is our time to arise to our full expression in Jesus' name. When I speak of full expression, I am saying that when we understand who we are in Christ, we will live out our full expression of who we are. Christ in you, the hope of glory! Colossians 1:27 We have yet to understand what we can do in Jesus' name, but if we allow God to work in us and through us, we'll find out.

A question I often get asked by women is "How do you keep rising up?" A couple of years ago, I read a book by Bobbie Houston titled *"I'll Have What She's Having."* What I got out of it is something that I will carry with me forever, as I journey into all of my seasons in life. She said that there will always be people who are running the race ahead of you, and there will also be people running the race behind you. As I read this, I came to a realization that what I am doing does affect the people running behind me, and the same goes for you. There are people ahead of you that are doing exactly what you're doing, and there are people behind you looking to you and wanting to do what you do. They are looking at our race, and if we quit or don't do our job, they may not do theirs. We have a responsibility to do our part and lead well because there are so many ladies that we are leading, that we can't slow down or quit. What encourages me are the people who are ahead of me in their races, who are paving the way for me to emulate and rise up to do my part. Women, whom I consider ahead of me, not just in age, but also in what they are doing for the kingdom. These women have made an impact in my life and have spoken truth and wisdom to me, as I arise to all that God has for me. Women such as Lisa Bevere, famous author and speaker, Bobbie Houston, Senior Pastor of Hillsong Church Sydney, Georgie Baxter, Senior Pastor of Enjoy Church in Melbourne, Australia, Leigh Ramsey, Senior Pastor of Citipointe Church in Brisbane, and Tina Archer, Senior Pastor of Foursquare Church in Washington, and so many others. I have learned and gleaned from them in many different ways. Watching them succeed and lead with their husbands has made a big impact on how I lead with my husband. They have modeled what a godly woman should be like, as well as how to be the wife of a senior pastor. Without these mentors in my life, I'm not sure where I would be today. I've changed over these past seven years of leading women through Arise. I've been challenged to rise up every day, to not give in to complacency and defeat. I had to overcome so many insecurities and fears, and battle the lies of the enemy every day until I could manage it. I had to be honest with myself about whom I believed I was or wasn't, and allow God to peel away the layers of lies, fears, and insecurities. I wanted to change because I believe I've been changed by the word of God. I wanted others to see that we are no different from one another. We are all the same, loved and adored by our Father in Heaven. We don't need to compare ourselves to one another, be critical or judgmental of each other, but we can be the best cheerleaders and encouragers toward one another. The ladies I've mentioned whom I look up to are women who are for me and not against me. You don't often find that in many relationships, especially in female relationships. But I want to break that curse in my generation and the generations to come. It's not about me anymore, but about my daughters and my granddaughters.

There were so many times that I asked the Lord, "Why am I leading Arise? When is the end date for this job? How much more rising up do I have to do?" But God said, "TAG, YOU'RE IT to lead these women, and there's more to come, so you're not done yet." Each time these questions went through my head, I had to change my perspective on how I saw things. I had to get back into the word and be encouraged to stay the course. And understand the *why* of what we do in helping women rise up to their full expression in Christ because so many have not risen. I'll be honest; I have these conversations with God at least a couple of times a year. I'll even have these conversations with my team because at times, I see them becoming complacent when it comes to planning the Arise conferences or other events that we have for the ladies. I often remind them why we do Arise and encourage them that they need to continue to arise as well. We can't lead women to rise up if we aren't rising up ourselves. I remind our team that we are in this together, forever, and we will arise together too.

As the leader of Arise, I literally had to take my position and walk in the authority that God has given me to lead. I realized this once I said, "yes!" at the Hillsong Colour Conference, when God spoke clearly to me about the 10,000 women worshiping in Hawai'i. I believe that day will come, but for now, I must not back down, slow down, or get complacent. I have more to do and I need to rise up.

What does walking in our authority mean? It means understanding who lives inside of you. When you accepted Jesus as your Lord and Savior, He came into your life and now dwells inside of you. Before Jesus died on the cross, He said that He would send us a helper, the HOLY SPIRIT, who will help us. As it says

> *"He is the Holy Spirit, who leads into all truth. The world cannot receive him, because it isn't looking for him and doesn't recognize him. But you know him, because he lives with you now and later will be in you."*

> **John 14:17 (NLT)**

I had to understand who lives in me because without the Holy Spirit, I could not lead the women. I need the Holy Spirit's help all the time! As God was changing me and helping me understand who I was in Christ, I was able to lead more confidently. I relied on God's grace every time I had to speak in front of people and as I led. Walking in my authority allows me to do all things in Christ who strengthens me.

> *"For I'm trained in the secret of overcoming all things whether in fullness or in hunger. And I find that the strength of Christ's explosive power infuses me to conquer every difficulty."* **Philippians 4:13 (TPT)**

I've tried leading in my own strength, and it didn't turn out the way it could have if I had relied on the Holy Spirit to help me. When I decided to take the position of leading Arise, I promised God that I would not lead in my own strength but with HIS, and God has been with me every step of the way.

I want to challenge you to take your position or assignment and be obedient to what God is calling you to do. It's time that you stand up and do your part in the kingdom. Stop looking to other women to do your job; it's your job to get it done. I remember when I decided to lead the women of our church, a woman came up to me and said, "We've been waiting for you to lead us." We have so much to do and not enough servants to do it. God has been nudging at you for a while to do something, and you've been running away and not listening. It's time you realize that you're not alone, and that God will help you to rise up to everything He wants for you. He needs a willing vessel to accomplish what He needs done on this earth. Let's be the women who will rise up because TAG, YOU'RE IT!

Chapter Twelve

PERFECTLY YOU

"Christ is our message! We preach to awaken hearts and bring every person into the full understanding of truth. It has become my inspiration and passion in ministry to labor with a tireless intensity, with his power flowing through me, to present to every believer the revelation of being his perfect one in Jesus Christ." Colossians 1:28-29 (TPT)

The Apostle Paul is one of my favorite pastors to be mentored by. I love the letters he wrote to the Galatians, Ephesians, Philippians, Colossians, and to Timothy. I get so encouraged every time I read these letters. I honestly feel like he is writing specifically to me. I love how he encourages and corrects the believers, and I especially love how he disciples people from prison through his letters. As I conclude this book, I want to do the same as Paul; I want to be an encouragement, as well as an inspiration, to each person reading this book. I want to awaken hearts and bring to you the full understanding of the truth about who we are in Christ and to realize that we longer have to be fearful, intimidated, or perfect. I want each of you to know that we all struggle to become exactly who Christ says we are: beautiful, accepted, honored, bold, brave, and loved.

In my connect group a woman named Ruby, said she's always felt that she was God's favorite, and ever since then, my entire group has been saying the same thing about themselves. I've come to a place in my life of understanding the truth about who I am and have found that intimidation, fear of rejection, and insecurities have really been Satan's way of distracting me from knowing my identity and from accomplishing all that God wants to do in and through my life. Satan will throw anything at us, even the kitchen sink, just to slow us down from knowing the full truth about who we are. Satan knows that once we know the truth about who we are, he no longer can mess with us. He will keep trying, but once you know the truth, you become aware of his tactics and schemes and will have wisdom and "fight words" to combat him.

When I know the devil is trying to intimidate me or cause me to question my identity in Christ, I'll say "fight words" like these in my head or out loud to him directly, "*YOU ARE A LIAR AND I WILL NOT ENTERTAIN THAT THOUGHT BECAUSE I AM A CHILD OF GOD WHO IS LOVED AND ACCEPTED, AND I MATTER TO HIM! NOW LEAVE ME ALONE AND GET OUT!*" You have to say it like you mean it. Don't talk sweet to the devil because he is not sweet to you. He wants to discourage and confuse you. I am a mom of three girls, and if anyone tries to hurt them, the mama bear comes out. I will not hesitate to scratch you or to tell you what I think about you. There is a righteous anger inside each of us that will not stand for any unrighteousness or harm to come near our children or our marriages. That's how we should be with the devil. And the biggest thing I had to remind myself of is that our God is a big God, and He is all-powerful and all-knowing, and He's got my back.

It's been quite a journey as I continue to rise up to my full expression in Christ. I no longer desire to be perfect, but to be perfected in Jesus. As I allow God to help me be aware of my insecurities and fears, God brings truth to those places. I've been very honest with God and with others because I want to be set free from those bondages. When you are set free from all of those insecurities and fears, you are allowing yourself to finally be exactly who God created you to be, *PERFECTLY YOU.* All of those fears and insecurities gave you a false image of yourself that caused you not to be you. When I realized this, my confidence grew. This confidence was not the kind of confidence you create for yourself, but a Godfidence that God gives. As you and I are assured of who we are in Christ, we will walk in a Godfidence that is healthy and pure. It's in His perfect love that we can trust God with everything and be perfectly ourselves.

> **16** *We know how much God loves us, and we have put our trust in his love. God is love, and all who live in love live in God, and God lives in them.* **17** *And as we live in God, our love grows more perfect. So we will not be afraid on the day of judgment, but we can face him with confidence because we live like Jesus here in this world.* **18** *Such love has no fear, because perfect love expels all fear. If we are afraid, it is for fear of punishment, and this shows that we have not fully experienced his perfect love.* **1 John 4:16-18 (NLT)**

As we go back to the book of Genesis with Adam and Eve, both were naked, and they were very comfortable with who they were. They walked the garden with such confidence and boldness; however once they sinned, they became aware of their nakedness and started to hide themselves and their insecurities. The serpent told them lies and brought fear to them. I want us to be naked before the Lord because this is where we will have that Godfidence and boldness to be exactly who God intended for us to be. Sin is still in the world, and we will continue to battle, but thank God for Jesus dying on the cross for us and forgiving all of our past and future sins. We are works in progress and grace allows us to rise up each day to our full expression in Christ. I love what Philippians 3:12-16 says:

12"I admit that I haven't *YET* acquired the absolute fullness that I'm pursuing, but I run with passion into his abundance so that I may reach the purpose that Jesus Christ has called me to fulfill and wants me to discover. 13I don't depend on my strength to accomplish this, however I do have one compelling focus; I forget all of the past as I fasten my heart to the future instead. 14I run straight for the divine invitation of reaching the heavenly goal and gaining the victory-prize through the anointing of Jesus. 15So let all who are fully mature have the same passion, and if anyone is not yet gripped by these desires, God will reveal it to them. 16And let us *ALL* advance together to reach this victory-prize, following one path with one passion." Philippians 3:12-16 (TPT)

Paul is encouraging us that we all have not *yet* acquired the absolute fullness, but we run with passion into His abundance so we may reach the purpose that Jesus Christ has called us to fulfill and wants us to discover. We haven't yet arrived at everything that God has for us, but we should pursue it all the days of our lives. We are being perfected in Him each day.

How do we be "perfectly you?"

First of all, **cling to God's word and live it out.** Don't just read and soak in the word, you have to act upon the word of God. *Philippians 1:20-21 (TPT)* " *20No matter what, I will continue to hope and passionately cling to Christ, so that he will be openly revealed through me before everyone's eyes. So I will not be ashamed! In my life or in my death, Christ will be magnified in me. 21My true life is the Anointed One, and dying means gaining more of him.*" To passionately cling means "with deep and intense yearnings." For example, my child used to cling to my leg for dear life each time I had to drop her off at the nursery. As we walked towards the classroom, she had her arm wrapped tightly around my legs, as she dragged herself to the class. We need to be like that with God. When we don't cling to God, we get lost and forget who we are, and that's when the devil begins to whisper lies in our ears and we begin to believe those lies. God wants us to cling to Him every minute of the day, even if we are having a hard day or a tough season. Never let Him go. As He is perfecting you day by day, the word is what will keep you focused.

As you rise up, you will be uncomfortable because God is stretching you. The stripping away of the old nature and old way of thinking, and the stirring up of gifts and talents in you can be very powerful. *Philippians 2:13 "For God is working in you, giving you the desire and the power to do what pleases him."* You may not like that process, but the process is necessary for your growth. As you go through the process, just cling to God and allow Him to take you where He wants to. Allow God to remove the things in your life that can be a distraction and to put the right things in your life instead. Your desires will turn to His desires for you, and that will lead you into the life that He wants for you.

The second thing is to stay *focused and strong*. Having vision is so important because without vision, people perish or run wild, as it says in Proverbs 29:18. God gives vision to His people, and it's up to them to obey and execute that vision. I also believe God gives vision to all of the senior pastors for the churches that they are called to lead. Mike and I have been shepherding Inspire Church for 15 years now, and it's been quite a journey for both of us, as well as for the teams of leaders that God sent to help us pastor this amazing church. Mike has always said that we not only pastor the people in our church, but the community that God has called us to, which is the 110,000 people living within the radius of our church. He doesn't just see the people who attend our services each weekend, but he sees the entire community as his flock. We don't have 110,000 people attending our church, but we will one day, because that's the vision God gave us. Within that vision, each of us, as leaders and members of the church, are to support and execute the vision. I believe the Arise ministry is part of that vision because of the growth we've had in the last seven years since we began Arise. Any time you build something that is in alignment with the vision, you will experience fruitfulness.

When you're on assignment from God, you need to stay focused and strong throughout the different seasons until God says you're done. Each year we host an Arise conference and several other events for the ladies. I have to say, I love leading Arise, but sometimes I wonder how long God wants me to do this. I guess this comes from wondering how much more passion and vision I have to keep this going. I love what it's doing for the ladies, and love seeing them rise up to their full expression in Christ, but I get concerned that this ministry can fall into complacency. As we plan each event and conference, I often ask my team, "What will be different from the last one?" I tell them to never take this for granted, and that we need to constantly stay focused on the vision and remain strong when we feel weak, bored, tired, or complacent. God often has to remind me why I lead the Arise ministry and why I do what I do each year for the ladies. It's because the women need to hear the truth about who they are in Christ. God called me to gather the women so that He could speak to them all at once. God knows I love people, and I love gathering people for a purpose because I want to do things with purpose. I believe God is speaking to ALL women around the globe, and He is calling us to rise up and be the generation of women that will be the answers to the problems of this world. I truly believe that we can make a difference right where we are at, in our homes, communities, schools, work places, and in the church. We are so gifted, and God wants to help us stay focused and strong to the calling upon our lives. God wants to change lives and help women to know that they matter to Him, and that He loves them so much. I know I can't quit or become complacent because God hasn't called me home yet, so that means I still have to finish my assignment. If you're reading this book, that means you're still alive, so that means you're either about to start on your assignment, or you need to be encouraged to stay strong and complete your assignment. Let's not quit; let's stay focused and strong.

Lastly, *you must RELAX!* What do I mean by that? Well, each time God stretches me, I don't like it; I often feel very tense because I'm uncomfortable, scared, and filled with anxieties. I get like this each time I have to share a message with the ladies or our church. At my last Arise conference, I remember being anxious about the message. You see, every time I prepare to speak in front of people, I feel anxious because I want to do well. I want to make sure that I have the correct message and am using the right scriptures and have the right illustrations to help communicate the message that

God has put on my heart. I go through this every time I have to get up in front of people. Finally, a good friend of ours, named David McCracken from Australia, told me that he had a word for me. He said that I needed to relax and not be so tense because when I am tense, the message can't be delivered. He compared it to giving birth – yes, a guy told me about birthing. He said when a woman is about to give birth, if she is too tense, she will have a hard delivery because her muscles are too tight. But if she is relaxed, she won't be tense and she will be able to deliver the baby smoothly. So, anytime you are being stretched beyond your limits or doing something that is out of your norm, try and learn to relax. When you are relaxed, you actually can be yourself. Usually when we are tense, fearful, or intimidated, we will have a hard time being ourselves because we aren't relaxed. So many of us worry about what others may think of us if we step out in our calling, whether or not that includes speaking, leading, or pastoring a church, because other people's approval is important to us. We all want to be liked, appreciated, and loved, and we want to perform well for others. But this is what causes us to lose focus, and we end up having anxiety, and then we can't be relaxed. As I said, we are at our best when we are relaxed. We can't have an epidural every time we want to relax because we are so filled with anxiety and fear. We need to trust in, rely and lean on Jesus to help us to relax so we can be perfectly ourselves. When you relax, you will enjoy the journey and it won't be as hard as it could have been. It can be very exciting to see what God wants to birth out of us.

We are all the called and chosen people of God to deliver His message of salvation and love. We all have an assignment to fulfill on this earth, so while we are still here, we need to find out what our assignments are and be obedient to finishing them. Allow God to stretch our capacity for the more that He has for us. Allow God to change us from the inside out, and don't hurry the process of change, but embrace each part of the process. We all have not arrived yet at everything that God has for us, but we press onward to that prize He has for us.

> **12-14** *I'm not saying that I have this all together, that I have it made. But I am well on my way, reaching out for Christ, who has so wondrously reached out for me. Friends, don't get me wrong: By no means do I count myself an expert in all of this, but I've got my eye on the goal, where God is beckoning us onward—to Jesus. I'm off and running, and I'm not turning back.*

> *Philippians 3:12-14 (MSG)*

I pray for all of us that we will hear the trumpet sound and be awakened to what God is doing here on the earth. God is calling us and wants our full attention. He wants to whisper things to you and give you strategies to fulfil the visions He has for you. He wants us to know who we are and what we are capable of doing because He lives inside of us. God said we can do all things in Christ, and we need to truly believe that we can.

I shared my story in Part One about where I came from and how embarrassed I was about being Chinese. Well, I can say with bold confidence now that I am a proud Chinese girl who was born in Hong Kong, and I have amazing, hard-working, and loving parents. I have finally come to a place in my life that I love being who I am: a Chinese Christian woman. I believe I am uniquely made, and I am very loved and accepted by my Father in Heaven. I have gifts and talents that my Father gave me to be used for His kingdom. I have a purpose and a destiny to fulfil while I am here on the earth. I can't waste a minute because every day is precious. I often go back to this passage in the bible in Romans 13:11-4 (msg) **11-14** But make sure that you don't get so absorbed and exhausted in taking care of all your day-by-day obligations that you lose track of the time and doze off, oblivious to God. The night is about over, dawn is about to break. Be up and awake to what God is doing! God is putting the finishing touches on the salvation work he began when we first believed. We can't afford to waste a minute, must not squander these precious daylight hours in frivolity and indulgence, in sleeping around and dissipation, in bickering and grabbing everything in sight. Get out of bed and get dressed! Don't loiter and linger, waiting until the very last minute. Dress yourselves in Christ, and be up and about!

We often need a kick in the butt to keep rising up, and I have to admit, I need a kick in my butt because I can be lazy and unmotivated. I need women in my life to kick my butt, and my mentor and big sister Lisa Bevere does that for me all the time when I hear her deliver messages to thousands of women. She fails to give in to complacency or laziness; she is always dressed and ready for battle. She won't give up on telling women that they need to rise up to everything that God has for them. We need a slap here and there and a swift kick just to be shook up enough to realize we can't fall asleep on our assignments. This same message is being spoken all over the world, and it's the same message I preach now as well. I am a member of those throngs of women that will take the gospel message by force to all those who will hear. I know my role and position now; I am to gather, equip, strengthen, empower, and mobilize the women through Arise.

This has been a journey, from the time I realized I wanted to do more in ministry after Charis was three years old, to hearing a life-changing message from John Bevere, to attending a women's conference in Sydney. My life has been changed for the better, and I'm so glad that I said "yes" to leading the women of Arise. I came to a place where I was finding myself again and learning about the lies that I had believed since I was a child, and how these lies cheated me on the life I could have had. I came to a place of accepting who I was and where I came from, and knowing that I am perfectly made in the image of God.

I hope this book has encouraged you in some way and has caused a shift in your spirit. You have to know that there is a calling and a destiny upon your life because you are God's child, and you have been given everything that Jesus was given and more. Jesus said we can do all things in HIM, and He meant it. He left us a helper, the Holy Spirit, who will guide us and help us with everything we need to do here on the earth. We are not alone, and we all have assignments to complete. Let's continue to encourage one another to finish the race that God has for us. Let's not quit or disqualify ourselves from this race. Let's stay awake and let's allow God to put His finishing touches on us. My greatest desire is that you would understand who you are in Christ, and that you would rise up to your full expression in Him because when you do, you will become all that Christ wants you to be, **PERFECTLY YOU**.